HUMAN RESOURCE MANAGEMENT ISSUES IN ACCOUNTING AND AUDIT FIRMS

Human Resource Management Issues in Accounting and Audit Firms

A research perspective

JOHN A. BRIERLEY
Sheffield University Management School
University of Sheffield, UK

DAVID R. GWILLIAM
School of Management and Business
University of Wales, Aberystwyth, UK

Routledge
Taylor & Francis Group
LONDON AND NEW YORK

First published 2001 by Ashgate Publishing

Reissued 2018 by Routledge
2 Park Square, Milton Park, Abingdon, Oxon OX14 4RN
711 Third Avenue, New York, NY 10017, USA

Routledge is an imprint of the Taylor & Francis Group, an informa business

A Library of Congress record exists under LC control number: 2001089123

ISBN 13: 978-1-138-70252-3 (hbk)
ISBN 13: 978-1-315-20976-0 (ebk)

Contents

Acknowledgements

This study was supported by a grant from the Centre for Business Performance of the ICAEW and we are grateful to the Centre for its support and assistance in particular to Anthony Carey and Richard Macve. We are also grateful to Arthur Andersen, Deloitte and Touche, Ernst & Young, KPMG and PricewaterhouseCoopers for their willingness to allow us to interview senior human resource management personnel in their firms. In addition, we are grateful for the assistance provided by the libraries of the University of Wales, Aberystwyth, University of Sheffield, University of Manchester, UMIST and Manchester Business School.

We should also like to thank the following people who commented on all or part of earlier drafts: John Ashman, Carl Chadwick, Pegi Gwilliam, Judith Hardy, Steve James, Richard Macve, Geoff Pye, Helen Williams and two anonymous reviewers on behalf of the Centre for Performance Measurement. Especial thanks go to Anwen Gwilliam for her assistance in the preparation of the camera-ready copy.

Executive Summary

Introduction

The rapid growth of accounting and audit firms over the last forty years, and in particular the transformation of certain firms into multi-national, multi-service providers employing many tens of thousands of staff, has given rise to recognition of the key importance of human resource management within these firms. There has also been an increasing awareness of the change in human resource management practice which has accompanied this transformation: and a questioning of whether existing models of staff management, organization and control are flexible and powerful enough to contribute to, and sustain, further development and growth.

In recent years there has developed, largely, but not entirely, in North America, a significant body of academic research into human resource management issues as they affect auditors and accounting and audit firms. The objective of this monograph is to present these research results in a manner which is both accessible and comprehensible to the interested reader.

The Audit Environment (Chapter 2)

The global commercial entities which the largest accounting and audit firms are today developed from modest beginnings in the nineteenth century. From the 1960s onward their growth has been spectacular and accompanying this growth was the adoption of a distinctive pyramidic staffing structure with concomitant high rates of staff turnover. In the last thirty years in the UK there has also been a transition from recruitment practices directed largely toward males not in possession of a university degree, to the situation today in which the great majority of new recruits are graduates and there is much more equality in the gender mix. Perhaps the most significant development in the last twenty years has been the tremendous expansion in the provision of services other than audit, for example taxation advice, corporate finance work, systems consultancy. In consequence, for none of the very large firms does audit work comprise as much as half of their overall fee income, and for some the proportion is much less than this. Recently, the desire to realize the economic value that has built up in activities beyond the field of accounting and audit has led to a number of large firms seeking to float or to sell off their consultancy operations. Notwithstanding this, it is likely that these firms will continue to be characterized by significant multi-disciplinarity in future years.

Features of the audit environment include: the diverse and contingent nature of audit assignments; the intense periodic time pressure under which auditors work; the constant requirement for accountability and review; the importance of the 'people' factor both within audit teams and in working with the client; the aspect of negotiation in the audit outcome. In recent years the nature of audit itself has been undergoing a transformation and its scope has expanded to include a range of assurance services beyond the traditional periodic audit of financial statements. This has led to a degree of convergence between the audit and the consulting role.

The Research Studies: Issues of Methodology and Generalisability (Chapter 3)

The majority of the studies reviewed in this monograph have been carried out in North America by academic researchers. In most of these studies the research design has entailed testing on a statistical basis for the existence of hypothesised relationships between variables of interest. The use of psychometric methods to provide measures of many of these variables, for example personality type, job satisfaction, raises questions as to the reliability and validity of these measures and of whether the myriad of factors that influence human aspirations, desires and well-being can be captured by measurement systems designed to ensure statistical tractability. Although the studies identify many statistically significant associations between relevant variables, the overall explanatory power of the models has typically been low. This suggests that they fail to incorporate many of the factors relevant to the human resource management issues that they are seeking to investigate.

The preponderance of US studies focusing on US auditors and US audit firms brings into consideration whether there are particular cultural, economic or institutional factors which might limit the transferability of the findings of these studies to the UK and other countries. There are substantial similarities between the commercial and economic environments within which the firms operate in the USA and the UK and there are also similarities in terms of the organization and structure of the firms themselves. However, there are some relevant differences. One of the most significant is that in the USA the formal teaching of accounting and associated subjects and the passing of professional examinations takes place ahead of joining an accounting and audit firm. In the UK approximately half of those recruited by accounting and audit firms will have no academic background in accounting or business and the possibilities for sitting professional examinations ahead of joining a firm have been very limited. In consequence the education process is interwoven with that of training and acculturation, and the professional examinations loom large in the early years of a career in an accounting and auditing firm.

The multi-service nature of accounting and audit firms and the various categories of professionals working within them raises questions as to whether there are differences in attitudes, behaviours and perceptions between accountants working as auditors and those working in other capacities, for example as taxation specialists or in mainstream consulting. If there are differences they may be relevant to the wider question of whether homogeneous personnel policies are appropriate across the firms or whether there should be variation across functional discipline.

Research Findings (Chapter 4)

We have sought to organize the reporting of the study results by reference to ten separate topic categorisations. Here for each topic we summarise the principal findings (these summaries are also reported in the main body of the text after each relevant section). It should be noted that in these summaries we are distilling and synthesising the findings of studies carried out over a time frame from 1970 onwards. In consequence, these summaries have to be interpreted in the context of the changes in accounting and audit firms that have taken place over this period as well as by reference to the caveats as to methodology and the generalisation of the results of US studies referred to above.

Personality and Needs (4.1)

- Individuals reaching senior positions within accounting and audit firms tend to possess strong masculine characteristics or a combination of strong masculine and strong feminine characteristics. Staff with strong feminine characteristics alone or without either strong feminine or strong masculine characteristics are less likely to reach senior positions.
- Individuals with greater needs for power and with less need for affiliation to other individuals are more likely to make a long term career in an accounting and auditing firm. Furthermore, they are more likely to enjoy higher job satisfaction and demonstrate greater organizational commitment.

Stress (4.2)

- Auditors are more likely to perceive themselves as attempting to reconcile irreconcilable objectives, for example ensuring adequacy of audit testing within a restricted time budget, in circumstances where the laid down command structure within the firm is by-passed or violated and where they perceive that relevant information is being withheld by more senior personnel in the firm. Role conflict is reduced when rules and procedures as to work practices and policies in the firm are formalised.
- Auditors are more likely to display uncertainty as to their appropriate role when the command structure within the firm is by-passed or violated. They are less likely to be uncertain of their role when superior personnel are receptive to suggestions for improved work practice and respond rapidly to problems put to them. Perceived role ambiguity is also reduced when the individual has the authority to take decisions and exercise responsibility.
- In those firms perceived as having a more structured approach to the audit task, role conflict is greater when the chain of command is by-passed or ignored. In firms perceived as having a more flexible audit methodology, role conflict is reduced by adaptability within the organization to changing circumstances, the ability of the auditor to take decisions and exercise responsibility, and the extent to which the auditor is provided with adequate information on a timely basis.

- In more structured firms role ambiguity is greater when the chain of command is by-passed or violated and when there are no set procedures for carrying out particular tasks.
- Auditors with a high need for achievement tend to suffer less work related stress.
- Role conflict contributes to job-related tension for male and female auditors. Role ambiguity contributes to job-related tension for female auditors alone.

Socialisation and Feedback (4.3)

- Newly recruited auditors obtain information about role demands and expectations, appropriate behaviours and attitudes and performance feedback indirectly from peers and from other members of the firm. In contrast, they are more likely to obtain technical information by means of direct enquiry of immediate supervisors.
- The extent to which newly recruited auditors engage in information seeking activities does not appear to have a very significant impact on the overall socialisation process.
- Appearance, manner and conduct, presentation to clients and integration with peers and superiors are important to the socialisation process.
- As auditors became more senior, immediate superiors appear to become a more important source for information as to job requirements and feedback as to how well the individual is meeting those requirements.
- Formal documentation, for example internal procedural manuals, are perceived by both seniors and managers as a relatively unimportant information source.

Career Development (4.4)

- In the USA a far greater proportion of entrants into accounting and audit firms possess a higher degree than is the situation in the UK.
- Auditors possessing a Masters degree, or having benefited from work experience with a public accounting firm in the course of their studies, are likely to be promoted to senior and manager more rapidly than those only possessing a first degree.

- Auditors perceive that females and unmarried auditors are less likely to achieve partnership. Personal attractiveness is seen as enhancing the chances of achieving partnership irrespective of gender.

Leadership and Mentoring (4.5)

- A number of leadership characteristics, for example consideration for the personal needs of subordinates, allowing staff innovation, the giving of frequent positive reinforcement, are positively associated with audit managers' perceptions of effective team performance.
- Audit seniors with dominant personalities tend to be more likely to ensure that subordinates know what is required of them within a clearly structured framework. They are also more likely to show consideration for the personal needs of their assistants.
- The satisfaction of audit assistants with their immediate work environment is positively related to the degree of consideration shown to them by the audit senior.
- When seniors provide a more structured work environment for junior staff it is less likely that audit juniors will sign off work that they have not in fact done. However, the underreporting of audit time increases in such an environment.
- There is mixed evidence as to whether a more considerate leadership style is associated with a reduction in the level of premature sign-off and other audit quality reduction acts.
- Mentor-protege relationships exist at all levels within firms but are particularly important at higher levels within the firm. The benefits to the protege include greater familiarity with practices, attitudes and modes of behaviour within the firm and the likelihood of accelerated promotion.
- Formal mentoring systems can be of benefit in assisting staff to make the transition to a new position and in terms of acquiring technical skills. Informal mentoring relationships are more likely to lead to greater self confidence and decision making ability in the protege.
- At lower levels in the firm high staff turnover, and the difficulties associated with ensuring interaction between the mentor and protege, limit the effectiveness of formal mentoring relationships.

Job Satisfaction (4.6)

- Factors which have been associated with enhanced job satisfaction include an initial intention to make a long term career in public accounting, a greater need for power than affiliation and a Type A (hard driving, aggressive, competitive and with a sense of time urgency) personality. Work-related stress is negatively associated with job satisfaction.
- Evidence as to the influence of role ambiguity and role conflict is mixed, but the majority of studies report that role conflict and role ambiguity have a negative effect on job satisfaction.

Professional and Organizational Commitment (4.7)

- Auditors with a greater belief in the existence and validity of absolute moral rules (idealists) display a greater commitment to, and involvement in, the accounting profession than those who believe that ethical considerations are essentially relative in nature.
- There is little direct association between auditors' level of idealism and their commitment to the goals and values of their organization, but there is a negative association between the level of relativism and organizational commitment.
- Managers and partners in firms with a less structured approach to audit display higher levels of organizational commitment than managers and partners in more structured firms.
- There is some evidence that the development of professional commitment precedes the development of organizational commitment. However, organizational commitment increases as individuals reach more senior positions within their firm whereas professional commitment does not.
- In the UK at least, for many junior employees professionalism and organizational commitment are virtually indistinguishable, both being couched in terms of dress, attitude and behaviour.

Staff Turnover (4.8)

- There is some evidence that auditors who possess an undergraduate degree alone have higher turnover rates than those with a Masters degree, but there is also evidence that other factors, for example the quality of the University attended, may have a more significant effect than the level of the degree alone.
- At more senior staffing levels female auditors are more likely to express an intention to leave the firm within a given time frame than males. At lower levels within the firm there is less evidence of differentiation between males and females with respect to turnover intentions.
- Turnover intentions of individuals are influenced by their long term career intention; their satisfaction with their job; the number of hours that they are prepared to work; as well as by a number of specific personality characteristics.

Performance Appraisal (4.9)

- There are differences between appraisers and appraisees within firms in respect to the importance placed on separate appraisal criteria, but there is little evidence that these differences are reflected in terms of perceptions of performance.
- At lower levels within the firm perceived technical skill is the appraisal criterion which has the greatest impact on performance evaluation. At higher levels within the firm technical skill assumes much less importance as a factor in performance evaluation.
- More systematic and structured appraisal systems, for example Behaviourally Anchored Rating Scales, allow a more complete indication of the factors determining the assessment of an auditor's performance and a more accurate assessment of that performance.
- Formal appraisal systems are only one aspect within a wider network of informal appraisal, assessments and relationships which feedback into an overall perception of an individual's performance and prospects.

Determinants of Job Performance (4.10)

- There is some evidence that auditors with educational qualifications at the Masters level and above perform better than those with undergraduate degrees alone, but the evidence is mixed. There is also evidence that at lower staffing levels performance ratings are higher when staff have experience of working in a public accounting firm while at university.
- As stress levels increase the job performance of individual auditors initially improves but beyond a certain level of stress measures of job performance begin to decline again.
- There has been extensive effort to seek to model the motivation and job performance of individual auditors by reference to their expectations that greater effort on their behalf will lead to greater rewards with value to them. To date these models, derived from the wider human resource management literature, have been relatively unsuccessful in their application to auditors.

Conclusions (Chapter 5)

Here we draw together on a thematic basis insights and observations derived from both the findings of the research studies reviewed and from a number of interviews with senior human resource management personnel in large accounting and audit firms.

Career Development

Certain of the individual attitudes and characteristics associated with success in accounting and auditing firms, for example above average needs for achievement and power, belief in one's ability to change things and to make things happen, are attitudes and characteristics which are traditionally deemed masculine in the organizational behaviour and psychology literature. A number of studies have highlighted the low proportion of women in the higher reaches of accounting and audit firms, as compared with the almost equal number of men and women who initially join these firms. Whether this is a consequence of a failure in human resource management within the firms or is a result of individual and societal characteristics largely beyond the control of the firms is less clear.

The process of acculturation and socialisation of new entrants to the firm is heavily influenced by learning from and observation of peers and immediate superiors and within an organizational ethos which places an emphasis on conformity to type. Because accountants and auditors in the large firms derive so much of their understanding of the term professional from the values and cultures pervasive in their firms it is debatable that the concept of being a professional has any meaning outside an organizational context. Other than in the setting of examinations, the professional bodies intrude little, if at all, in the process of professionalisation.

Although there has been persistent questioning within the firms as to the economic efficacy of the pyramidic staffing model and the associated high levels of staff turnover, it has proved to be resilient and still forms the basic staffing pattern in the large firms today. However, there are signs of change including: recognition of the value of employing and training personnel for alternative qualifications, for example AAT qualifications; a greater willingness to recruit personnel at all levels instead of relying almost exclusively on the career progression of trainees; a greater flexibility of career pattern, including the possibility of longer term careers within the firms for those not achieving partnership or equivalent status. The pyramidic staffing structure has essentially been a construct of audit and the partnership pattern of ownership and control. As other functional areas within the firms assume ever increasing importance, and as the management structures within the firms converge with those of other large commercial entities, it is likely that this staffing pattern will be increasingly open to challenge.

The Multi-Disciplinary Global Firm

Today's large accounting and audit firms are conglomerates which provide an array of professional services, some cognate some disparate, on a world wide basis. This confronts human resource management with the task of accommodating the particular ways of doing business within the various functional areas, while simultaneously controlling tensions between these areas and resisting pressures for break-up and demerger. Analogous problems arise as a consequence of globalisation. Here the need to maintain an equivalent quality of practice and service might suggest an essential uniformity of human resource management practice and procedures within a firm on a worldwide basis. However, to date, the clear differences in the commercial and cultural environments in the different countries within which the firms operate mean that there have been significant problems in operationalising common practices.

Internal Management and Structure

The increasing importance of 'management' as a function in its own right within accounting and audit firms gives rise to the possibility of tension between the providers of professional services and those who seek to manage and organize that provision. In accounting and audit firms the locus of power and control is still retained by partners, or those with an equivalent status, emanating from a client service background. Professional management, as for example in the professionalisation of the human resource management function within the firms, has grown in status and profile, but as yet the direct link between client contact and the revenue and profitability of the firms means that internal credibility and power still resides with those individuals who are, or who have been, 'client facing'. This contrasts with the situation in the education and health services where the link between the service providers and income is much more diffuse and professional 'management' has assumed far greater importance and power.

However, the firms have embraced enthusiastically management concepts in terms of the setting of targets and rewarding the successful achievement of these targets. At more senior levels within the firms, the internal culture is focused heavily on the attainment of short term performance goals, a culture driven in part by the overriding imperative for growth. Failure to exceed or at least match the growth of competitors is seen as likely to result in the loss of status and clients and threaten the long term survival of the firm as an independent entity.

Research Directions

Many of the studies reviewed in this monograph have focused on human resource issues of direct interest to accounting and audit firms, for example investigation of the link between prior educational achievement and subsequent career development, but their impact on human resource management practice in the UK has been minimal. In part this is explicable in terms of the North American orientation of many of the studies undertaken, in part because many of the studies are now quite dated, and in part because the main ambition of the studies has been academic publication rather than direct relevance to practice. We would advocate a greater emphasis on the study of human resource management issues in accounting and auditing firms from a wider sociological and organizational perspective. This might entail study of how the unusual recruitment patterns and staffing structures of the large firms have contributed to and interacted with their sustained growth into the phenomenon which the global professional services firms are today. It might also examine the role of these firms in providing large numbers of UK graduates with experience of the wider commercial environment and the world of work.

1 Introduction

For accounting and audit firms,[1] the management of their staff, or as an economist might phrase it their human capital, is a key aspect in their successful and profitable operation. Staff, or human resource, management involves issues relating to recruitment, acculturation, learning and training, job satisfaction and morale, incentives and promotion, retention and departures. It also entails considerations as to work practice, organization, scheduling, decision making and lines of authority within firms, international liaison and integration. Because of the nature of the operations of accounting and audit firms, human resource management issues are inextricably tied up with those of power and control within the firm, issues that have increasingly come to the fore since management, as a function in its own right, has emerged as a powerful force within these firms.

Recognition of the importance of human resource management and change in the manner in which it is accomplished within accounting and audit firms have accompanied, and to an extent been a response to, the transformation of certain of these firms from entities relatively modest in size and clearly grounded within a distinct profession to the global colossi of today. A transformation which many would say has meant that they have outgrown the symbiotic relationship with the accounting profession which characterised the development and growth of these firms. The extent to which such changes, for example the adoption of the pyramidic staff structure or, more recently, the adoption of 'new' management practices and discourses,[2] have been a Darwinian response to competition and change in the market for audit services is itself an interesting question. If

---

[1] Although the usual descriptor of those firms which provide auditing services, and frequently a wide variety of accounting and advisory services also, is that of accounting firms, in this study the term accounting and audit firms is normally used, reflecting the fact that the primary focus of this monograph is on human resource management issues as they relate to auditing. On occasion and according to context the North American terminology of public accounting firms is employed.

[2] Dirsmith *et al.* (1997) document the rise of management by objectives within the large North American public accounting firms.

this were so then one would expect human resource management practices to be reasonably homogenous at least across classes of accounting and audit firms. However, there are differences within the large firms in their approach, for example with regard to recruitment policies, the size of operating group, standardisation of audit practice within the firm, levels of specialisation, the ratio of partners to professional staff, management practices and structure within the firm etc. These differences are still more marked when the small and medium sized firms are brought into the comparison.[3]

The perceived differences between firms, and a more general recognition of the importance of the underlying issues, have given rise to interest in whether there is a role for more formal investigation and research in assisting accounting and audit firms, large and small, in developing their human resource management strategies and policies. In the US context, Belkaoui (1989) called for such research in the following terms:

> the primary asset of the certified public accounting firm is its professional staff. The success of the firm depends on motivating them, retraining them and keeping them satisfied. Research on human resource considerations in public accounting firms is therefore necessary in order to identify the factors that create the ideal atmosphere for members of accounting firms to function efficiently and be satisfied with their jobs.[4]

A number of commentators, for example Dirsmith *et al.* (1997), Anderson-Gough *et al.* (1998), have echoed this call for further investigation and research.[5] In fact over the last quarter of a century there has developed, largely, but not entirely, in North America, a significant body of academic research into human resource issues as they affect auditors and accounting and audit firms. As noted in Chapter 3, the

---

[3] To take a specific example in terms of the cost of training student accountants, one large London firm has estimated that over the years of their training contract students earn positive returns to the firm of up to £10,000 (although see p.85 below for a more gloomy assessment of the economics of training student accountants in large firms). In contrast a small regional firm with lower charge-out rates estimated that students cost a net £10,000 to train (Boyer, 1995).

[4] p.115.

[5] Dirsmith *et al.* (1997, p.5) suggest that the large accounting firms represent 'the most under researched organization based profession to emerge as a direct consequence of commercial enterprise.' Anderson-Gough *et al.* (1998, p.29) note that 'there has been remarkably little study of the recruitment, training and socialization of accountants.'

approach, focus and methodology of much of this research has resulted in its publication in a form and in journals which are not necessarily immediately accessible to UK readers. The principal motivation underlying this monograph is therefore to collect together the results of these research endeavours, to present them in a manner which is both accessible and comprehensible, and to provide a suitable bibliography and referencing for the interested reader who wishes to return to the original source material. Encompassed within this ambition is a desire to illuminate more clearly the nature of human resource management issues as they affect auditors and accounting and audit firms, to discuss the contribution and value of the research that has already taken place, and to identify avenues along which future research might most profitably be directed.

The methodology that we have used in our endeavour to achieve these goals is that of a literature review based on publications in relevant accounting, auditing, organizational behaviour and psychology research journals. Details of the journals from which the primary source material was drawn are set out in the Appendix. There have been previous literature surveys covering aspects of human resource management within accounting and audit firms, for example those of Ferris and Dillard (1988), Belkaoui (1989), Dillard and Ferris (1989), Parker *et al.* (1989) and Hunt (1995). This study is not intended to replace these invaluable pieces of work, which are themselves directed toward an academic audience, but does have the ambition of updating, widening access and perhaps increasing perceptions of the relevance of the research carried out to date. There have also been a number of 'meta-analysis' studies which have sought to draw together on a statistical basis the results of separate research endeavours within a related field.[6] In contrast to these, this study seeks to employ qualitative research review techniques in order to provide an understanding of the research methods employed and the variety of results obtained.

In any literature review of this type there is a tension between the extent to which the review is an exercise in categorising, reporting and, where appropriate, synthesising the methodology, findings and results of the studies surveyed, and the extent to which it is sought to critique and interpret the ambitions and outcomes of these studies. While not eschewing traditional patterns of categorisation and reporting, this study has sought to place the research work that has taken place within a wider

---

[6] See Brierley (1998a,b,c; 1999a,b; 2000a).

contextual and environmental background and in so doing has perhaps leant closer toward aspects of critique and interpretation than previous surveys. Inevitably interpretation cannot be divorced from the perspectives, viewpoints and perhaps prejudices of the co-authors,[7] but it is hoped that the potential gains, in terms of making the work both more readable and useful, outweigh any potential loss in terms of objectivity and rigour.

To aid our understanding and exposition of the environment and space within which human resource management articulates itself in accounting and audit firms we also conducted a small number of unstructured interviews with senior personnel holding human resource management responsibilities in accounting and audit firms. These interviews were invaluable in providing clarification and insights most notably into the changing notion of accounting and audit firms and the major human resource management implications of these changes. We are grateful to the individuals concerned for giving up their time to talk to us and to their firms[8] for encouraging them to do so.

Beyond this introductory chapter the monograph is structured as follows:

Chapter 2 provides an essentially contextual background focusing on the nature of auditing and of accounting and audit firms, the auditing environment and the environmental factors which affect human resource management within accounting and audit firms. As such it identifies both explicitly and implicitly a number of the issues to which research either has been or might be directed.

Chapter 3 examines the way in which research to date has been carried out, highlighting methodological strengths and weaknesses. In that the great majority of the studies reviewed are of North American origin, there is consideration of whether the results and findings of these studies are transferable to the UK and international environment. There is also discussion of whether there are significant differences in human resource management terms between auditors, other staff of accounting and audit firms such as taxation specialists and management consultants, and accountants in general.

---

[7] Both of whom, at differing points in time, participated in the acculturation and socialisation process attached to qualifying as a chartered accountant with a large accounting and audit firm (albeit not the same firm).

[8] These were Arthur Andersen, Deloitte & Touche, Ernst & Young, KPMG, and PricewaterhouseCoopers.

Following a brief introduction, Chapter 4 seeks to report and interpret the results of the published research under the following headings:

Personality and Needs
Stress
Socialisation and Feedback
Career Development
Leadership and Mentoring
Job Satisfaction
Professional and Organizational Commitment
Staff Turnover
Performance Appraisal
Determinants of Job Performance

At the end of each section there is a short summary of the principal research findings reported.

Chapter 5 draws together, on a thematic basis, certain of the research findings and highlights a number of possible directions for further enquiry and investigation.

The Appendix sets out for those studies reporting results specific to auditors details of the sample size and coverage and the level of seniority of the individuals studied. The Bibliography includes the references to the studies contained in the Appendix together with references to other research studies focusing on human resource management issues relating both to auditors and accountants more widely defined. It also includes the additional references contained in the main text and the footnotes thereto.

2 The Audit Environment

Auditing and Accounting and Audit Firms

The term auditing covers a panoply of activities and concepts. These include: operational audit; performance audit; internal audit; public sector audit; environmental audit; as well as the traditional external audit of company financial statements.[9] This study focuses on the human resource issues underlying the provision of audit services by private sector accounting and audit firms, services which may encompass all of these activities and others, although for most firms periodic financial audit will provide the greater part of their audit related fee income (but not necessarily the majority of their overall fee income).

Specialist accounting and audit firms emerged in the UK in the nineteenth century and began to flourish in the latter part of that century as education, population, commerce and trade all expanded apace.[10] These firms were relatively small, even a major firm such as Price Waterhouse had only four partners and fifty seven employees at the turn of the century. Organizational routines were in keeping with the size of these enterprises, for example the four Price Waterhouse partners met every morning for about half an hour to deal with post, allocate new work and record the receipt of fees, while all staff had to report every morning on work in progress.[11]

A parallel development in the second half of the nineteenth century saw the professionalisation of accounting. The Institute of Chartered Accountants in England and Wales (ICAEW) was formed in 1880 and rapidly grew to achieve pre-eminence among the various professional associations formed then and subsequently. Initially membership of the ICAEW was open to those experienced in accounting but it quickly moved to ensure that all new members qualified by means of passing a series of

[9] See Power (1994, p.1) for a taxonomy of various types of audit and Power (1997) for a description of the extended role of audit in society today.

[10] Parker (1986) provides an overall perspective on this growth. Previts (1985) traces the development of the profession in North America.

[11] Jones (1995) p.79.

examinations[12] as well as serving an appropriate period of training, 'articles', within an accounting firm. Although it was not until 1948 that there was a statutory requirement for company auditors to possess professional qualifications, it was by then extremely rare for a company of any size to have an unqualified auditor. Subsequent legislation has made little attempt to limit the powers of the professional bodies with regard to the licensing of auditors and, in its capacity as both a Recognised Supervisory Body and a Recognised Qualifying Body, the ICAEW still plays a dominant role in this respect. Other UK professional bodies with similar powers, but each with a significantly smaller number of members, include: the Institute of Chartered Accountants of Scotland (ICAS); the Institute of Chartered Accountants of Ireland (ICAI); and the Association of Chartered Certified Accountants (ACCA).

The twentieth century saw dramatic changes in the size and scope of operations of the larger accounting and audit firms both within the UK and on an international basis. Auditing today has become a world-wide activity and the large firms all have international umbrella organizations overarching and overlooking the activities of the various national firms (although typically these national firms still possess a significant degree of autonomy). The 1960s saw the emergence in North America of the 'Big Eight' firms.[13] The 'Big Eight' were characterised by similarity of size and scale of operations (which were significantly larger than those of any other accounting and audit firms) and their transnational nature. However, even within the Big Eight there were differences (for example, Arthur Andersen, founded much later than the others, focused heavily on consultancy, whereas Price Waterhouse was notable for its blue chip audit portfolio) and at a national level outside the USA the relative size and importance of the individual firms varied.[14] In the 1980s a distinction developed between those firms which embraced a more quantitative and structured approach to auditing and those which adhered to a more flexible judgement based approach.[15] In recent years this distinction has largely

---

[12] The first examinations were held in 1882.

[13] These were: Arthur Andersen; Arthur Young McClelland Moores; Coopers & Lybrand; Deloitte Haskins & Sells; Ernst & Whinney; Peat Marwick Mitchell; Price Waterhouse; and Touche Ross.

[14] For characterisation of perceived differences between the Big Eight firms see Stevens (1991).

[15] See Cushing and Loebbecke (1986), Kinney (1986) and Turley and Cooper (1991) for discussion of actual and perceived differences in audit methodology. Bowrin (1998)

disappeared[16] although individual firms still seek to claim advantages in audit technology and in delivering value to their audit clients.[17] The last twenty years has seen a reduction in actual and perceived North American hegemony as the audit markets in Europe and the Far East have grown in importance. They have also seen the Big Eight reduce to a 'Big Five'[18] as a result of a series of mergers.[19]

The scale of operations of the Big Five firms is now very far removed from that of their forebears at the beginning of the twentieth century. In 1900 Price Waterhouse generated £30,718 in fee income in the UK. Ahead of the July 1998 merger, the constituent parts of PricewaterhouseCoopers generated an estimated annual UK fee income of £1,324m.[20,21] At its inception, the UK staff of the new firm totalled 16,443 (including approximately 1,000 partners). On a worldwide basis fee income was $13,130m,[22] there were 140,000 staff (8,979 of whom were partners) operating in 152 countries. Although PricewaterhouseCoopers are currently the largest international firm, even the smallest of the Big Five, Arthur Andersen (now Andersen), generated worldwide fee income of US$8,400m for 1999/2000.[23] Until checked by the recession of the early 1990s, the large UK accounting and audit firms had enjoyed almost continuous growth in both fee income and staff since the early 1960s. Not only did their size increase spectacularly during this period, but there were also major changes in terms of the employment profiles of the firms and the qualifications of the staff that they recruited.

---

reviews the research literature focusing on structural and organizational differences between accounting and audit firms.

[16] Bowrin (1998, p.64) suggests that all the firms which now comprise the Big Five currently adopt a semi-structured approach to audit.

[17] For example, in the UK Ernst & Young has Audit Innovation, KPMG has Audit 2000. See *Accountancy*, June 1998, pp.84-5 for a discussion of whether the differences in approach are genuine or whether they are primarily driven by marketing considerations.

[18] These are: Andersen; Deloitte Touche Tohmatsu; Ernst & Young; KPMG; PricewaterhouseCoopers. In the UK Deloitte Touche Tohmatsu operates under the name Deloitte & Touche.

[19] There are frequent references in the text to the 'Big Six' reflecting the position which had held for nearly a decade ahead of the merger of Price Waterhouse and Coopers & Lybrand.

[20] *Accountancy Age*, 30 July 1998, p.12.

[21] Two years later this had risen to an estimated £1843.3m, *Accountancy Age*, 6 July 2000, p.14.

[22] *Accountancy*, September 1998, p.14. For the year ended 30 June 2000 this had risen to $25,500m (*Accountancy*, February 2001, p.8).

[23] *Accountancy*, February 2001, p.8.

Perhaps the most significant change was the almost universal adoption of a pyramid staffing structure and a route to partnership within the firm taking between 10 and 15 years.[24] Whereas in the past being an audit clerk or an audit manager could be a career in itself (almost half the employees of Price Waterhouse in 1936 had been with the firm for more than 10 years)[25] this was no longer possible and those not achieving partnership were not expected to stay within the firm.[26] This staffing structure entailed both a large intake of trainees on an annual basis and a commensurate turnover of staff in the years after qualification. Again, until the early 1990s, the market for qualified accountants was such that this turnover could be achieved very largely on a voluntary basis. The downturn of the early 1990s both affected the income of the accounting and audit firms and also greatly reduced the opportunities available to qualified accountants in the wider job market. These two factors contributed to the wave of forced departures from the large and medium sized firms, an unprecedented phenomenon which prompted firms to re-examine the suitability of their recruitment practices and of the pyramid structure itself. However, as yet, any adjustments to the staffing pattern have been modest rather than dramatic and, as the economy improved in the middle half of the 1990s, the recruiting levels of the large firms returned to the levels reached at the end of the 1980s. Since its formation PricewaterhouseCoopers has claimed to be the largest graduate recruiter in the UK and plans to take on 1350-1400 graduates in 2001.

This staffing structure is not necessarily unique to accounting and audit firms and is paralleled, to a lesser extent, in certain other professions, for example architecture and law. It is nevertheless a highly distinctive feature and in no other profession are the numbers employed in individual firms so large or, arguably, is an 'up or out' policy so ruthlessly employed. While it possesses clear advantages in terms of generating a high degree of internal competition within an environment where the rewards to success are considerable[27] there are also potential disadvantages. In few other fields

---

[24] Robson *et al.* (1996). Hull and Umansky (1997) suggest that in the USA it takes on average twelve years for a newly recruited staff accountant to achieve partnership.

[25] Jones (1995) p.166.

[26] As Anderson-Gough *et al.* (1998, p.74) note: 'The patently pyramidical hierarchies of the firm illustrate that in order to be successful within the firm one has to move up the hierarchy or move out.'

[27] For the year ended 30 September 1998, KPMG UK highlighted the 'overall reward' (made up of a combination of executive income and proprietorship profit) per partner as £305,000. The average number of partners in the year was 587 and in total 574 partners

are firms prepared to invest so extensively in training and yet retain staff for such a relatively short period of time. Excessive competition for advancement within firms may promote dysfunctional behaviour and leave the firm exposed on quality grounds. Rapid staff turnover and the use of inexperienced staff on audit assignments may irritate clients.[28] Audit itself may be becoming more skilled and specialist and technology may be capable of reducing the need for labour intensive checking and vouching. Although in the past individuals within firms have moved into specialist areas having trained in general audit practice this too may not be appropriate as these other specialisms become increasingly important within firms. The rigid hierarchical structure imposed by progression from junior to senior grade and then through various categories of manager before achieving partnership may also have disadvantages compared with a flatter and more open structure.[29]

This itself highlights another significant change in the structure of the profession. Whereas in 1969 university graduates formed less than 20% of the 4,232 admitted in that year as student members of the ICAEW, by 1984 they comprised more than 85% of the then student intake of 5,171, and today less than 10% of those admitted to training contracts do not possess a degree.[30] Again the large firms were the leaders in graduate recruitment and had effectively moved to an all graduate intake by the 1980s. However, graduates with a degree in a commercially orientated subject, for example in business or management studies, only constitute approximately half of the student intake overall and within this group a still lower proportion are 'relevant' graduates - relevant in the sense that their degree studies wholly exempt them from foundation stage examinations of the professional accounting bodies.[31] Another significant change lay in terms of the growth of the number of female entrants to the

---

received executive remuneration in excess of £100,000 (KPMG UK Annual Report 1998, p.1 and pp.41-42). For the year ended 30 September 2000 the average income per partner was £417,000 and the income of the UK senior partner exceeded £1.6m (KPMG UK Annual Report 2000).

[28] Hermanson *et al.* (1995).

[29] See Hawksley (1995) for a description of the manner in which Coopers & Lybrand sought to reduce the hierarchical structure within the firm. In the UK, Ernst & Young make some claims to have a more informal and flatter organizational structure than the other large firms (Perrin, 1997).

[30] Whittington (1995), ICAEW (2000).

[31] The recent restructuring of the ICAEW examination system has reduced the importance of the relevant/non-relevant distinction.

accounting profession. In the thirty years from 1964 to 1994 the number of women admitted to ICAEW membership increased from less than 2% of the annual total to 35%[32] and in the large firms women now constitute almost half of the student intake. Their representation at the highest levels of these firms and in particular at partnership level is still however quite small (as is that of ethnic minorities).[33]

Although this monograph is primarily focused upon research into human resource issues as they relate to audit and to auditors in accounting and audit firms, it is impossible to overlook the dramatic growth in other services offered to clients some of which are far removed from the traditional focus on accounting and auditing. Ahead of recent demerger activity for none of the Big Five firms did fees derived directly from audit comprise more than half of their overall fee income and until the divorce of the accounting/audit and the consulting arms more than three quarters of fee income of Arthur Andersen came from services other than auditing. These non-audit services include taxation advice, corporate finance work and a range of consultancy activities with an emphasis on systems and information technology consulting. These services are provided both to audit clients and to others, although the evidence suggests that in the UK at least, the greater part of non-audit service fee income still derives from audit clients.[34] Accounting and audit firms have always provided services beyond audit but the rapid development of these sectors of activity in recent years has contributed to a change in the outside perception of the activities of these firms, and also possibly to a shift in cultural attitudes within the firms themselves. Differential patterns of growth and profitability have also caused organizational stresses, as typically overall authority and control in the firms has been retained by those emanating from a background in audit and accounting rather than consultancy.

---

[32] Whittington (1995), by 1999 women represented 43% of the overall student intake (ICAEW, 2000). See also Ciancanelli *et al.* (1990) and Boyer (1995).

[33] Jones (1995) p.340. In the wider context, Hammond (1997) documents the effective exclusion of African Americans from the US profession until the 1960s and their continuing under-representation in the profession. Today African Americans comprise 12% of the population of the USA but constitute approximately 1% of the total number of Certified Public Accountants (CPAs). For a discussion of this issue in the UK context see Fisher (2000) who notes that non-whites made up 8.9% of the ICAEW student intake in 1999/2000.

[34] *Accountancy*, October 2000, p.10 suggests that for clients int the FTSE 350 only 30% of accountancy and audit firms' fee income derives from statutory audit.

In recent years there have been quite dramatic structural changes as certain of the very large firms have sought to dispose of all, or part, of their consulting businesses. The long running and acrimonious divorce between Arthur Andersen (now Andersen) and Andersen Consulting (renamed Accenture from 1 January 2001) was finalised by means of a legal settlement in August 2000. In this settlement the International Chamber of Commerce rejected the claim by the umbrella organization Arthur Andersen Worldwide that Andersen Consulting should pay $14.5 billion as a penalty for breaking away.[35] KPMG which had already seen Cisco Systems invest $1 billion in the KPMG internet services business raised $2 billion in a flotation of KPMG Consulting in February 2001.[36] Earlier in 2000 Ernst & Young spun off its consulting business to the Paris based management consulting and information technology group Cap Gemini for $12.4 billion.[37] In February 2000 PricewaterhouseCoopers announced an intention to devolve its consulting practice and corporate finance activities. Later in the year it took part in negotiations with Hewlett Packard with a view to a possible $17 billion acquisition by Hewlett Packard of PricewaterhouseCoopers' global management and information technology practice,[38] although Hewlett Packard subsequently withdrew from these negotiations.[39]

Audit Engagements

Each audit engagement has distinctive features according to the particular characteristics of the client and the terms of the audit engagement. Relevant client characteristics include: size, the activities in which it engages, the nature of its accounting and information systems, reporting requirements and deadlines. For corporate entities industry factors will be important; the audit of a financial institution is likely to be very different from the audit of a similar sized manufacturer; the entity may be a group with hundreds of subsidiary and associated undertakings or may comprise just one 'stand alone' company; its operations may be confined to one

[35] *Accountancy*, September 2000, p.7.
[36] *Accountancy*, September 2000, p.8, *Accountancy* March 2001, p.10.
[37] *Accountancy*, October 2000, p.8.
[38] *Accountancy*, October 2000, p.8.
[39] *Accountancy*, December 2000, p.8.

location or spread across almost any number of locations in the UK and world-wide.

However, although each audit is different there is an essential similarity in the manner in which the great majority of financial audits are conducted. Financial audit under the UK Companies Acts entails the gathering and evaluation of sufficient evidence to enable the auditor to form an opinion as to the truth and fairness of the financial statements prepared by the client company. This evidence can itself take a variety of forms and guises: evidence as to the competence and integrity of the client personnel; evidence as to the proper functioning of systems of control within the company; evidence confirming the existence and proper valuation of assets and liabilities etc. The basic evidence gathering process is normally the responsibility of a team of field auditors working at the client company. The number and seniority of the staff that constitute this team is very much dependent upon the size and complexity of the client, but on the typical medium sized audit the team would normally contain a mixture of junior unqualified staff and more senior staff who are about to qualify or have recently qualified. For smaller audits the field audit team may consist of one or two auditors, perhaps a junior and a senior based at the client for typically one, two or three weeks, whereas for the audits of multinational companies the field audit team will be very much larger and may well be led by staff at managerial level based at the head office of the client for a period of months rather than weeks. However, for many of these clients the variety of activities and locations means that there will be a number of much smaller field audit units operating at some or all of these locations.

Whatever the size of the engagement, the work of each field audit team will be subject to review by managers within the firm and ultimately by the engagement audit partner responsible for the client.[40] Toward the end of the annual audit and depending upon the nature of the financial statements and the evaluation of the evidence gathered there may then be a period of negotiation normally at manager/partner level with the client. These negotiations will usually centre on potential adjustments to the financial statements based on differing opinions and interpretations relating to accounting policies, estimated figures etc.

Although some forms of evidence can be gathered at any time in a client's financial year, for example assurance as to the underlying quality and strength of the client's accounting and information systems, the bulk

---

[40] Work carried out within the field audit team may first be reviewed by the leader of the field audit team.

of the field audit work normally takes place immediately before and immediately after the client's financial year end and, typically, as the reporting deadline approaches, time pressure develops both for the field audit team and for those involved in negotiations with client management. These pressures are frequently exacerbated by delays in the preparation of the accounts and supporting schedules by the client. An example of the extent of the negotiation process and the time pressure can be seen in the 1989 BDO Binder Hamlyn (joint) audit of a security alarm company described as a 'middle-ranking client' of Binder Hamlyn. As noted below, this audit led to subsequent litigation[41] and in his description of the audit the judge noted that:

> There were meetings on 4, 7, 8 and 9 October 1989. The final audit clearance meeting was on 9 October 1989. The final consolidation was not received until 7pm on Thursday, 5 October 1989. This meant that there was intensive work to do between then and Tuesday, 10 October 1989 when the preliminary group results were to be announced.[42]

At the meeting on Sunday 8 October 1989 there were at least 22 items of suggested amendment under discussion - but the client service partner did not appear to find this to be particularly unusual, arguing that 'auditors are used to working under pressure'.

Audit or Assurance Services?

The picture sketched out above is one of the conventional audit of financial statements but for the large firms today financial audit is seen as just one element, albeit a very important one, in a range of 'assurance services'. Assurance services can encompass a wide range of activities[43] in which the role of the audit firm is that of adding credibility to assertions made.[44] A Special Committee of the American Institute of Certified Public

---

[41] *ADT Ltd. v. BDO Binder Hamlyn* [1996] BCC 808.
[42] Ibid at p.813.
[43] A survey of 21 large and medium sized firms carried out for the AICPA Special Committee identified over 200 separate non-audit assurance services being provided by these firms (Elliott, 1998).
[44] The AICPA Special Committee used as a working definition 'independent professional services that improve the quality of information, or its context, for decision makers.' (Elliott, 1998, p.2).

Accountants (AICPA, 1997) identified six areas of existing assurance services which the Committee considered to have particular potential for future growth:[45] assurance as to the business practices and integrity of electronic commerce providers; assurance as to the quality of health care provision; assurance that systems are designed and operated to provide reliable information; risk based assessment of the likelihood and magnitude of adverse events; assurance as to the quality of provision for the elderly; assurance as to the relevance and reliability of entity performance measures.

Another facet of the change in the audit process has been an extension in the scope of financial audit to include much wider consideration of aspects of strategic risk and business planning. Jeppesen (1998) refers to this expansion of the scope of audit as a 'reinvention' of audit and suggests that whereas 'the old audit was confined primarily to the financial statements, the new audit approaches attempt to audit the auditee's entire business and strategy.'[46] Furthermore, he suggests that the focus on risk and strategic objectives has led to a blurring of the traditional distinction between auditing and other services provided by the accounting and audit firm: 'To some extent auditing has become consulting and it makes increasingly little sense distinguishing between the two as the boundary between them is eroded by the 'reinvention' of auditing.'[47,48]

Contingency and Accountability

The audit environment is a highly contingent one for the employees of accounting and audit firms, particularly those below managerial level. Auditors constantly have to adjust to different physical locations and patterns of travel; clients with different activities, personnel and systems; different groups of fellow auditors; periodic episodes of extreme pressure of work etc. However, it is also a strongly hierarchical environment and one within which staff at all levels may perceive themselves to be

---

[45] The Committee's ball park estimates were that the provision of these services would double or even quadruple the US profession's level of accounting and auditing revenues over the 'next several years' (Elliott, 1998, p.6).

[46] p.525.

[47] p.526.

[48] This view was echoed by a North American large firm partner who stated: 'there is a continuum in the whole audit advisory services area. I don't think it's any more possible to define discrete breakpoints.' (Boritz and Cockburn, 1998, p.142.)

constantly accountable (through the need to account via time sheets for each hour, or sub-division thereof, of work) and their work to be subject to continual review and monitoring. This review takes two forms: the checking and questioning of their work as part of the evidence gathering and evaluation process, and the system of staff reporting whereby auditors below managerial level are normally subject to reports on their performance on each assignment which themselves input to more formalised periodic review procedures.

Continual review is one facet of a process of training and acculturation within firms - a process designed *inter alia* to present a uniform, positive, image to actual and prospective clients, to generate *esprit de corps* and an identification with the firm amongst the staff, and, perhaps most importantly, to ensure a uniform standard and quality of audit work. At partner level the consequences of inappropriate or faulty decisions and judgments can be devastating. Although the effective destruction of a medium sized firm by the actions of a single 'rogue' partner, as happened in the 1980s to the Australian firm of Fell and Starkey, is extremely rare, the litigation between ADT and BDO Binder Hamlyn illustrates the enormous potential liability that can arise out of what was essentially a routine business meeting attended by just one quite junior audit partner.[49] At lower levels of the audit, a besetting concern for audit firms is to ensure that requisite audit procedures are in fact carried out appropriately. The possibility that audit personnel will claim to have carried out procedures when they have not in fact done so is enhanced by the enormous pressure placed on all levels of the audit staff to carry out work within designated time budgets, and also by the fatigue and strain that can develop toward the end of an audit assignment. Although the review process is typically detailed and thorough, it is extremely rare for it to involve an element of reperformance and therefore it may fail to prevent such behaviour.

Contingency, complexity and uncertainty are not confined to auditors: they also pervade the environment within which those responsible for the management of human resource issues operate. As was seen in the early 1990s, when economies experience downturns staffing and recruitment plans and strategies built around a high level of voluntary staff mobility may have to be revised accordingly. At other times economic upturns may

[49] At first instance damages of £65m plus interest were awarded against BDO Binder Hamlyn, the court holding that there had been a voluntary acceptance of a duty of care to a third party with respect to an audit opinion negligently given. A settlement, reported at £50m, was subsequently agreed between the parties.

require premiums being paid, to buy in qualified staff who have not trained with the firm, which may itself entail problems of acculturation, integration and retraining. Some areas of work, for example corporate finance, insolvency and aspects of consultancy, are more cyclical and unpredictable than others, and judgements have to be made as to the extent to which additional staff should be recruited and trained when activity is high, and as to how far staff levels should be reduced when it is low. Another factor is that clients are now more likely to change auditors than before and this may have significant effects on work loads in either direction. The pattern of audit work is not spread evenly, a high proportion of large companies have 31 December year ends and traditionally in the UK the later part of the summer has been a very quiet period. To some extent this is compensated for by the ability to use staff interchangeably on audit and non-audit engagements, but this may be limited by the need for particular specialist skills for services outside audit which junior audit staff do not possess. During their training period students require time to study and prepare for their professional examinations. Failure of students to pass the examinations (which may in part be the result of excessive pressures of work[50]), or indeed their failure to complete their training contracts for whatever reason, is costly. Forward allocation and scheduling of staff to audit assignments is fraught with uncertainty as individuals may leave, fail professional examinations etc.

---

[50] Although a recent empirical study (Brierley, 2000b) did not find any evidence of a relationship between workload and examination performance.

3 The Research Studies: Issues of Methodology and Generalisability

The Nature of the Research

This monograph focuses primarily, but not exclusively, on research carried out by researchers based in North American universities. Of course there are far more academic researchers within the accounting discipline in the USA,[51] but there are also differences in the relationship between the academic community and accounting and auditing firms in the two countries and in perceptions of the value of this type of research. UK firms have traditionally been much less willing than their US counterparts to provide research sites for academic researchers, although here there have been signs of change in recent years.[52] It is also arguable that UK academic researchers have been less attracted to the type of behavioural research with a strong statistical underpinning, within which genre the majority of studies reviewed in this monograph fall, and relative to US researchers a much smaller proportion have been trained in the application of the methodological techniques necessary to carry out such studies.[53,54]

---

[51] Steele (1983) estimated there to be approximately 300 academic accountants in UK universities as compared with 5,800 in the USA. Although the research active academic accounting community in the UK has grown in number since the early 1980s, it is still an order of magnitude smaller than that in the USA.

[52] For example Anderson-Gough *et al.* (1998) were given extensive access to trainees at two large UK accounting and audit firms in their study of socialisation processes within firms.

[53] For a more detailed discussion of differences in the US and UK approaches to auditing research see Gwilliam (1987, pp.25-30).

[54] Evidence of a more specific interest in human resource management issues as they relate to accounting and audit firms in the USA may also be seen in the existence of monthly publications such as the *CPA Personnel Report* and the publication in North America of the book *Recruiting and Retaining Accounting Professionals*.

Few, if any, of the authors of the ninety-six papers detailed in the Appendix are practising professional accountants, although a significant number of the studies proceeded with the active collaboration and support of accounting and audit firms. This support has taken a number of shapes and guises including financial assistance, access to staff on training courses, and encouraging staff to respond to questionnaires.

The great majority of this research has been published in journals which require some form of refereeing process, normally by other academics. As such they are part of the exponential growth of research in the social sciences in general, and accounting and auditing in particular, in recent years. This dramatic upsurge in research activity has been accompanied by questioning as to the value of such research.[55] Cowton (1999) identifies concerns as to *timing* (the time lag associated with research and publication diminishes the contribution of the insights obtained, if indeed the problem being addressed is still a relevant one), *lack of comprehensibility* (the use of specialist language which may amount to little more than obfuscation); and, irrespective of the speed and comprehensibility of the research, a *general lack of practical application and relevance.*

One factor which may underlie this lack of practical application is a refereeing process which focuses on rigour in the research design and on methodological innovation, rather than on either the relevance of the research topic or the value of the results obtained. The importance of publication in key journals to the career development and status of academic researchers cannot be overstated and is likely to far outweigh any concerns as to the direct applicability of the results. Furthermore, replication studies and indeed works of summary and synthesis are perceived to be less likely to attract the interest of journal editors and referees.

The emphasis on statistical validity and rigour is clearly illustrated in the fact that of the ninety-six papers identified as researching human resource management issues specifically in the auditing context only five employ no formal statistical testing. The overwhelming majority use some form of parametric statistical tests, on occasion in combination with non-

---

[55] For example, Lee (1995) suggests that accountants have failed to provide a convincing explanation of either the current role of academic research or of its relative isolation from the world of practice. The quite extensive literature which has grown up around this question includes Dent *et al.* (1984), Hopwood (1988), Bell and Wright (1995), Gwilliam (1995), Swanson and Gross (1998).

parametric testing.[56] The essential underlying methodology employed, with variations, by many of these papers is to hypothesise relationships between certain constructs based upon prior theory and then to test for the existence of these hypothesised relationships. A typical example of such a methodology is the study by Rasch and Harrell (1990) as illustrated in Figure 1.

Figure 1: (Adapted from) Rasch and Harrell's (1990) model of the impact of personal characteristics on the turnover intentions of accounting professionals

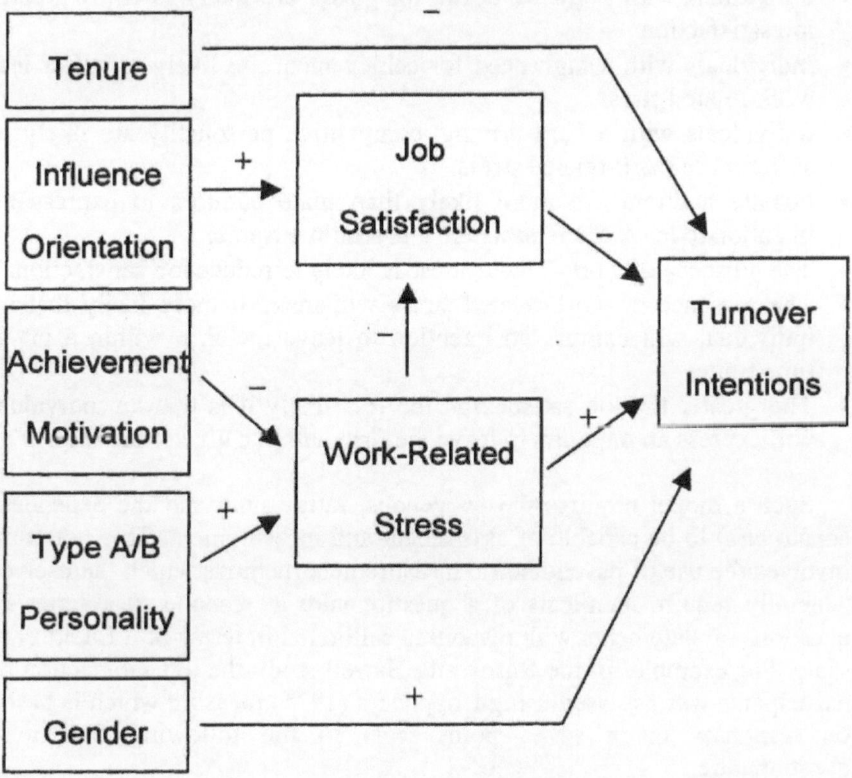

[56] Sixty-three use parametric tests alone, twenty-four use a combination of parametric and non-parametric tests, four use non-parametric tests alone.

This cross-sectional model focuses on the manner in which a variety of personal characteristics (the exogenous constructs in the model) are expected to influence the existence of work related stress and the extent of job satisfaction (the intervening constructs in the model) and ultimately the intention to change employment (the dependent construct in the model). From the model the following direct effects are identified

- The longer an individual has been working with their firm the less likely they are to express an intention to leave the firm within a given time frame.
- Individuals with a greater desire for power are likely to enjoy greater job satisfaction.
- Individuals with a high need for achievement are likely to suffer less work-related stress.
- Individuals with a hard driving, competitive personality are likely to suffer more work-related stress.
- Female auditors are more likely than male auditors to express an intention to leave the firm within a given time frame.
- The presence of work-related stress is likely to reduce job satisfaction.
- The presence of work-related stress will make it more likely that an individual will express an intention to leave the firm within a given time frame.
- The greater the job satisfaction the less likely it is that an individual will express an intention to leave the firm within a given time frame.

Such a model requires the exogenous, intervening and the dependent construct(s) to be capable of assessment and measurement. This normally involves the use of psychometric measurement methods which themselves generally require recipients of a questionnaire to respond to a series of questions or statements with responses calibrated in terms of a Likert type scale. For example, in the Rasch and Harrell study the job satisfaction of participants was assessed using Hoppock's (1935) measure which is based on responses on a seven point scale to the following four item questionnaire.

a) Which one of the following shows how much of the time you feel satisfied with your job?
1. Never.
2. Seldom.

3. Occasionally.
4. About half of the time.
5. A good deal of the time.
6. Most of the time.
7. All the time.

b) Choose the one of the following statements which best tells how well you like your job.
1. I hate it.
2. I dislike it.
3. I don't like it.
4. I am indifferent to it.
5. I like it.
6. I am enthusiastic about it.
7. I love it.

c) Which one of the following best tells how you feel about changing your job?
1. I would quit this job at once if I could.
2. I would take almost any other job in which I could earn as much as I am earning now.
3. I would like to change both my job and my occupation.
4. I would like to exchange my present job for another job.
5. I am not eager to change my job, but I would do so if I could get a better job.
6. I cannot think of any jobs for which I would exchange.
7. I would not exchange my job for any other.

d) Which one of the following shows how you think you compare with other people?
1. No one dislikes his/her job more than I dislike mine.
2. I dislike my job much more than most people dislike theirs.
3. I dislike my job more than most people dislike theirs.
4. I like my job about as well as most people like theirs.
5. I like my job better than most people like theirs.
6. I like my job much better than most people like theirs.
7. No one likes his/her job better than I like mine.

The scoring of responses on a seven point scale (from one to seven) allows a measure of job satisfaction to be achieved by simple summation of responses over the four questions with the highest level of satisfaction having a score of twenty eight and the lowest a score of four.[57]

In the Rasch and Harrell study the majority of the other constructs are measured in a similar fashion. Influence orientation and achievement orientation are measured by the Job Choice Exercise (Harrell and Stahl, 1981,1984), Type A/B personality by a twenty item measure developed by Glazer (in Goldberg, 1978), work related stress by a fourteen item scale developed by Rizzo *et al.* (1970), and turnover intention more simply on a two point scale.

Reduction of the various constructs of interest to researchers to number form makes it possible to test on a statistical basis for the existence, or otherwise, of the hypothesised relationships. In that the majority of studies test the impact of a number of exogenous constructs upon one dependent construct, ordinary least squares (OLS) multiple regression, or variants thereof, can be used. OLS multiple regression seeks to establish how much of the overall variation in a particular construct of interest can be explained by the combined effect of a number of other specified constructs. Furthermore, it allows determination of which of the constructs are themselves significantly affecting the outcome. In its simplest form the overall predictive success of the model is determined by the coefficient of determination R^2,[58] whereas the contribution of the individual exogenous variables is determined by their βs and (and this is the factor of most importance in the majority of studies) whether their effect in the model is a genuine one or whether it is the product of random statistical variation. This latter question, that of whether the variable is 'significant' in the statistical sense of the term, is essentially tested in terms of the likelihood that the results obtained could be obtained by chance alone and is normally reported in terms of a significance level, 1%, 5%, or sometimes 10%. Put simply, significance at the 1% level suggests that if the test was run one hundred times then it would be expected that on one occasion the same result would have been obtained as a result of random statistical variation, notwithstanding the absence of any genuine association between the variables.

---

[57] Frequently the total score is rescaled, in this case by means of division by four, to give an overall score ranging between one and seven.

[58] The R^2 measures the proportion of the variation in the dependent construct that is accounted for by the independent construct(s).

In the Rasch and Harrell study a variation of the basic OLS methodology is used. Path analysis allows the estimation of direct and indirect effects between a number of constructs where causal ordering has been specified in advance. In the Rasch and Harrell model the direct effects (or path coefficients) are the standardised regression coefficients (βs) obtained from the OLS multiple regression runs for work-related stress, job satisfaction and turnover intentions. From the direct effects it is possible to calculate the indirect effects of constructs upon either job satisfaction or turnover intentions. For example, the proposed indirect effect of influence orientation on turnover intentions is the product of the βs between influence orientation and job satisfaction, and between job satisfaction and turnover intentions. In other words it is the effect of influence orientation on turnover intentions through job satisfaction. The indirect effect of achievement motivation on turnover intentions is the product of the βs between achievement motivation and work-related stress and between work-related stress and job satisfaction and between job satisfaction and turnover intentions (or the effect of achievement motivation on turnover intentions through work-related stress and job satisfaction), plus the product of the βs between achievement motivation and work-related stress, and between work-related stress and turnover intentions (or the effect of achievement motivation on turnover intentions through work-related stress).

More recent studies have extended analysis of models similar to that of Rasch and Harrell described above by means of the use of structural equation modelling software packages such as LISREL, EQS and AMOS.[59] These packages not only calculate direct and indirect effects between a set of constructs, but also correct for measurement error (in terms of lack of reliability in the responses received) and identify the best fitting model from a number of different models.

Issues of Measurement and Methodology

The reduction of the constructs to numerical measurement by means of responses to a limited number of pre-ordained questions is itself

[59] Gregson (1992a), Joreskog and Sorbom (1993). Morrison (1993a) is an example of a study reviewed in this monograph in which the covariance structure model methodology underlying LISREL is applied using LISREL software.

problematic. Responses may be driven by differing interpretations of language and culture.[60] They may be driven by perceptions as to what the 'right' answer should be, particularly where respondents are very new to a firm or where the questionnaire is answered in the context of a group training programme. Respondents may give high scores for attitudes perceived as desirable, such as job satisfaction, but low scores for behavioural intentions likely to be perceived as undesirable, for example an intention to leave within a short time horizon.[61] Respondents may systematically misrepresent themselves for other purposes[62] and the spread of responses across a seven point scale may be influenced by a desire to avoid extreme values. More generally, the subtlety and variety of the myriad factors that influence human aspirations, desires, well being etc. may not be brought out by a measurement system designed to enable statistical tractability. Perhaps even more fundamentally, many social thinkers (for example, Winch, 1958; Habermas, 1978; Chua, 1986) would argue that human beings are not natural scientific objects because the structures that exist around them are created and interpreted by them. In consequence, attempts to measure particular attributes or perceptions within the framework of these structures are theoretically flawed and likely to lead to misleading and erroneous results.

Concerns as to the reliability and validity of the measurement methods used are not new and many of the psychometric measurement methods used have been subject to check as to their reliability and validity. Reliability is seen in terms of whether the same results will be obtained if the test is used repeatedly on identical subjects, whereas validity relates to whether the measure actually measures what it purports to measure. Whereas questions of reliability are primarily empirical ones, questions of validity are to some extent semantic ones. For example, if a measure shows that subjects express a high level of intention to leave but in fact staff turnover is low does this indicate that the measure used to determine intentions is not a valid one, i.e. the staff do not have a desire to leave?

---

[60] Maupin and Lehman (1994, p.431) justify the use of an instrument designed to measure characteristics of femininity and masculinity on the grounds that it measures social stereotypes 'operative in our organizations, manifested in our personal lives, promoted in the mass media' rather than that it provides any genuine categorisation.

[61] For further discussion of the phenomenon of social desirability response bias see Crowne and Marlowe (1964).

[62] Hull and Umansky (1997) suggest that the provision of responses perceived as 'politically correct' may be a particular problem in gender based research in accounting and auditing.

Instead it may mean that the staff genuinely believe that they intend to leave but do not translate this into action, or that they intend to and try to leave but are unable to secure other employment.[63]

Although the great majority of the studies use, with varying degrees of sophistication, similar statistical methodology, both the methodology and the interpretation of the results have been open to question. One fundamental statistical issue is whether the collection of data by reference to an ordinal scale makes that data, taken singly or in aggregation, inappropriate for the statistical purposes to which it is put.[64] One advantage to researchers from the use of data collected in this form is that, in appearance at least, it rarely violates the underlying distributional assumptions on which the validity of OLS and OLS related hypothesis testing are dependent.[65] However, some econometricians would argue that the use of OLS and OLS type testing on raw ordinal data is inappropriate in these circumstances because the calculated means and variances which form the basis of OLS and OLS type methodology are themselves meaningless. Appropriate transformation of the data may make possible completely different results in terms of predictive ability and significance.[66]

Other concerns relate to the low overall predictive power of many of the models used, and the focus on statistically significant results for individual variables[67] rather than on the overall explanatory power of the models used. The low explanatory power of many of the models does

---

[63] For further discussion of the issues of reliability and validity see Litwin (1995). For a more general review of the literature pertaining to construct measurement issues in behavioural accounting research see Kwok and Sharp (1998).

[64] Cohen and Cohen (1983) point out that strict adherence to the underlying regression assumption that all variables are measured using interval measurement, that is with equal intervals between each point on the measurement scale, would prevent the use of this methodology for almost all psychological testing as these tests use ordinal data. Ordinal data, for example that derived from Likert scales, differentiate on a scalar basis and it is not usually possible to say that the difference between each point is equal. However, Cohen and Cohen consider that when the inequality between scales is small then this is not likely to adversely affect the validity of multiple regression analysis.

[65] For example, whereas in empirical work using company financial data problems of multi-collinearity, heteroscedasticity and non-normality of the distribution of the residuals are ever-present concerns they rarely even warrant a mention in the studies reviewed in this monograph.

[66] See Bond *et al.* (forthcoming, 2001).

[67] See Lindsay (1995) for a critique of what he considers to be an inappropriate fixation on significance testing in behavioural accounting research.

suggest either that they are failing to capture factors which are systematically important, or that the heterogeneity of individual perceptions and responses is such that overall models are of limited value. There are also issues as to causality and as to the degree of interdependence and circularity between the variables. For example, there is an abundance of evidence that there is a positive association between organizational commitment and job satisfaction but it is less clear whether people are satisfied in their job because they are committed to the organization or whether people are committed to the organization because they are satisfied in their job.[68]

As can be seen by reference to the Appendix both the sample size and method of selection have varied widely across the studies. In many of the studies the sample size is below one hundred and on occasion below fifty, in others the sample consists of many hundreds and on occasion over one thousand. Some studies focus on just one office in one firm, others on multiple offices across a range of firms. The great majority cover one or more Big Eight/Big Six firms, some also include (US) national/regional/local firms, although few, if any, focus on small or medium sized firms alone. Sample selection is rarely completely random in that most studies proceed with the co-operation of the firm whose staff are under study and sample selection is often tailored to fit in with training courses (at which the questionnaire instruments can be administered). Response rates too vary. In those studies which have proceeded with the active support and encouragement of the firms involved, participation and response rates have been very high, in others based on 'cold' mail questionnaires the response rate has been much lower.

The widespread reliance on measurement and statistical inference in the studies reviewed in this monograph has perhaps resulted in insufficient emphasis being placed upon other methods of enquiry and research. There have been few studies which have made use either of interviews or of more widely based case study methodology.[69] What such research methods may lack in terms of statistical rigour may be compensated for by a greater richness in the manner in which they reflect the perspectives of individuals and the complex environments within which they work. There have been

---

[68] See p.81 below for further discussion of this issue.

[69] A notable exception in the UK context is the Anderson-Gough *et al.* (1998) study. This study also provides, pp.36-42, an interesting discussion of wider issues relating to research in the social sciences and the strengths and weaknesses of various methodological approaches.

one or two studies in which the methodology has included participation in or shadowing of the work of auditors and audit teams, but these have been rare.[70] The majority of studies have been cross sectional rather than longitudinal in that they have focused on measuring perceptions and attitudes at a particular point in time rather than on comparisons between surveys done at differing points in time or on tracking cohorts of employees through time.[71]

In the great majority of the studies the focus has been on relatively junior staff members.[72] The pyramidic staffing structure means that junior staff significantly outnumber senior staff and acculturation and the development of attitudes to work may be presumed to be at their most significant in the initial stages of employment with an auditing firm. Furthermore, it is arguable that because of the unusual staffing structure and *modus operandi* of accounting and audit firms the human resource management issues of interest are those in relation to junior staff. However, human resource management is important at all levels within a firm. How are managerial staff identified as being suitable for partnership? At what stage are staff counselled that they are unlikely to achieve partnership? How have managerial structures adapted to reflect the dramatic growth in the size of firms? It may be that the research focus on junior staff and on field audit teams at the expense of issues relating to more senior staff has been disproportionate.

The Transferability of the Results of US Studies

As in other areas of accounting and auditing research, the dominant perspective in human resource management research as applicable to accounting and audit firms has been North American. The overwhelming majority of the studies reviewed in this monograph are by US authors and use as subjects of study US auditors and audit firms. This does bring into consideration the question of whether there are particular cultural, economic or institutional factors at play which might limit the

---

[70] Where this has taken place the shadowing has normally been at partner level, see for example Baker (1977), Dirsmith *et al.* (1997).

[71] There have been exceptions, for example Dirsmith *et al.* (1997) is a large sample, interview based, longitudinal study focusing upon senior personnel.

[72] Typically staff below manager level.

transferability of the findings of these studies to the UK or to other countries.

In many ways the similarities between the accounting and audit environments in the UK and the USA far outweigh any differences. The Big Five which, with one exception, share Anglo-American roots are established as colossi in both countries. In both countries there is a supporting structure of medium sized firms and small practices. The commercial and legal environment within which these firms operate shares many common features, as of course does the wider cultural and political milieu. However, within, and to an extent underlying, these similarities are areas of difference which may be relevant to the issues under question.

One significant difference lies in the educational experience and qualifications of entrants to the accounting profession. In the USA almost all of those recruited into audit will have an educational background which includes a significant element of accounting. The uniform CPA examination may be taken before graduation and most new recruits will have taken the examination ahead of joining their firm. Whereas in the UK for all those recruited into training contracts, with or without relevant degrees, 'the examination process assumes a central and important place in the trainee's experience of training',[73] in the USA it looms much less large within the work environment. Recruits into US firms will normally possess a substantial prior knowledge of accounting and audit from an academic/theoretical perspective, whereas in the UK new recruits whose academic background contains a significant element of the study of accounting and audit are in a minority. In both countries possession of a Bachelors degree is the normal educational qualification, but a significantly higher proportion of entrants into US firms are likely to possess a Masters degree.

There may too be differences in the manner in which the profession and a career in accounting and audit are viewed. Arguably, the status of the profession and the professional firms has been higher in the UK than the USA. This may be a reflection of a different approach to professionalism and the nature of the professional,[74] or it may be rooted in differences in class structure and their reflection in the world of work. The UK tradition

---

[73] Anderson-Gough *et al.* (1998, p.96).

[74] In the USA qualification and licensing as a CPA is a state prerogative and CPAs do not have to be members of the American Institute of Certified Public Accountants.

of paying a premium to train with a firm was not paralleled in the USA,[75] and although this distinction has long since gone it may be that the high proportion of recruits to the large firms from the more prestigious, traditional UK universities, most notably those of Oxford and Cambridge, suggests that at least vestigial traces of this class association remain.[76]

For more than a century labour practices in the US have been seen as more flexible than those in the UK, flexible in the sense both of a greater willingness of employees to move between jobs and also of a greater willingness of employers to move on or dismiss staff. There is some evidence that this carries through into the market for accounting professionals. In their longitudinal study Harrell and Eickhoff (1988) classified almost one third of new recruits who left within thirty months of joining a large public accounting firm as 'involuntary departures'.[77] Although UK firms are now more prepared to make staff redundant both within and outside training contracts it is doubtful whether the level of involuntary departures is as high in the UK as it is in the USA.

A final difference that we identify is geographic in nature. In the UK, London is both the capital and the commercial centre. It is in the London offices of the large firms in the UK that economic and executive power resides. In the larger US economy no one city or region now dominates to the extent that London still dominates the UK commercial environment. However, in the past, perhaps because of their relatively small size, many of the regional offices of the large firms in the UK possessed quite significant autonomy - although in recent years the trend has been for greater centralisation of power. Whether because of the greater geographical and economic size US firms have felt it necessary to impose tighter management structures[78] or whether there is greater diversity in the

---

[75] Articled clerks paid a substantial premium, 500 guineas, in order to train with Price Waterhouse in the UK in the inter-war period - they received no salary. Predominantly from a public school background they were treated as a privileged class (Jones, 1995, p.167). Until 1939 jobs at Price Waterhouse were not advertised, staff being engaged on the basis of personal introduction (Jones, 1995, p.226).

[76] Anderson-Gough *et al.* (1998, p.57) reported that only four of their sample of 77 trainees in the regional offices of two Big Six firms had graduated from the 'new universities' (i.e. former polytechnics).

[77] Involuntary departures were defined to include both staff who were asked to leave and staff who would have been asked to leave if they had not first resigned. However, the time frame within which this latter group would have been asked to leave was not clearly specified.

[78] Dirsmith *et al.* (1997) document the pressures for more centralised management structures within large US public accounting firms.

human resource management practices across the offices of US firms are open questions.

Accountants or Auditors?

Much of the research that has been carried out into human resource management issues as they apply to accounting and auditing firms is derivative, in the sense that it is based on research studies originally to be found in the organizational psychology literature which have been adapted to the accounting and auditing environment. There has also been research reported in the organizational psychology literature which has used accountants as subject material. In many of these studies the research has included within its scope accountants in general rather than being confined to auditors. This orientation raises two further questions. The first is whether the results reported add to our knowledge of human resource management and of the attitudes and perceptions of employees in organizations generally; or whether they add to our knowledge of human resource management issues as they affect the accounting and audit profession, and of the attitudes, perceptions and behavioural intentions of accountants and auditors *per se*. The second question relates to whether there are differences in human resource management terms between auditors and other categories of professional staff within accounting and audit firms, for example those working in taxation or management consultancy.

With regard to the first question, from one perspective any research that adds to our knowledge of human resource management issues also adds to our knowledge of human resource management in the accounting and auditing context, irrespective of the context in which this knowledge is gained or for what immediate purpose. However, from a practical viewpoint it may be that studies which are focusing on a particular attitude, perception or style of management and for which accountants merely form accessible and convenient research subjects, have less to contribute to our understanding of human resource management issues, as they impact accountants and accounting and audit firms, than those studies which focus more directly on the issues as they affect accountants and within the context of the work of accounting and auditing firms.

The question of whether accountants, more widely defined, share similar attitudes, behaviours and perceptions with auditors as a separately identifiable group has received some research attention. The question is an important one from the perspective of accounting and audit firms for whom the non-auditing aspects of their activity are becoming increasingly significant. Are differing personnel policies appropriate for separate groups of employees within the accounting and audit firms?

The importance of distinguishing between various parts of an organization was highlighted by Jiambalvo *et al.* (1983) who stated:

> [a] consequence of the segmentation of the organization into parts is that the behaviour of organizational members will be influenced by the segmentation. Because of differences in the nature of the task, and in the environmental uncertainty facing various segments, organizational members will develop different mental processes and working styles, adopt different decision criteria, and may have varying perceptions of reality.[79]

Benke and Rhode (1980) suggested that there were indeed significant differences between personal attributes and levels of job satisfaction of auditors, taxation personnel, and management consultancy staff working for accounting and audit firms. In particular management consultants were more sociable and outgoing than audit and taxation staff, a finding which they attributed to the need for management consultants to sell their services directly as compared with audit and taxation which, then at least, was seen as more of a captive market. Management consultants had a less bureaucratic orientation than audit and taxation staff and were more likely to undertake unpaid overtime or travel time. Another significant difference was that management consultancy staff were less likely to be satisfied with their level of promotion or the quality of their supervision than audit and taxation staff, but conversely were more satisfied with their remuneration. On this basis Benke and Rhode noted:

> There seems to be little justification for treating higher level professional employees of large CPA firms as a homogeneous group. Large CPA firms should be cautious about extending personnel policies from audit and tax sections to MS *(management services/consultancy)* sections. Policies that are well-received and useful in audit and tax may not be well accepted in MS. Also researchers that treat audit, tax and MS specialists as a homogeneous group may arrive at erroneous conclusions. Care should be taken to ensure that the sample is homogeneous with respect to the variables measured.[80]

---

[79] p.16.
[80] p.199.

Differences were not confined to auditors and taxation staff as one group and management consultants as another. There were different determinants of job satisfaction as between audit and taxation staff and this led Benke and Rhode to conclude:

> CPA firms should not assume that policies aimed at increasing the level of job satisfaction (and, hence, reducing turnover) among audit specialists will necessarily have the same effect among tax specialists....researchers of the job satisfaction of higher level employees in large CPA firms should treat audit, tax and MS separately. Failure to do so may obscure positive results or lead to erroneous conclusions.[81]

Jiambalvo *et al.* (1983) too found differences between these three groups in the context of how they made performance evaluation decisions. In a study utilising methodology developed in clinical judgement research, they found that the relative importance of different dimensions of performance evaluation varied - in the decision making processes of seniors, managers and partners - as between audit, taxation and management consultancy departments. The differences lay primarily between the taxation personnel and those in the other two groups, as differences between auditors and management consultants were small. They suggest that their results may be attributed to greater team orientation in the work of audit and management consultancy departments in contrast to the more individualistic nature of taxation work.[82]

In the UK, Craner and Greenfield (1995) found there to be some significant differences in measures of role conflict, role ambiguity[83] and

---

[81] p.199. This conclusion was reinforced by Benke and Rhode (1984) who found variations in the determinants of the turnover intentions of these three types of accountant.

[82] Conversely, Pratt and Beaulieu (1992) suggest that it is the culture of the management consultancy departments which differs from that of the audit and taxation departments. In the UK too Jones (1995) suggested that in Price Waterhouse the greater similarity lay between the culture of the audit and the taxation departments buttressed by the fact that approximately half of the tax practitioners trained initially in audit. In contrast the dependence of management consultancy on unique and non-recurring work and the decreasing proportion of consultants who trained in audit had led to the development of a different style and culture. From a gender perspective Coutts and Roberts (1995) report a higher proportion of women carrying out what is perceived as lower status auditing and taxation work whereas the more prestigious consulting and financial services are male dominated.

[83] See p.49 below for definitions of role conflict and role ambiguity.

job satisfaction between audit, taxation insolvency and management consultancy staff of the provincial offices of large UK accounting and audit firms and concluded that:

> The evidence...suggests that the social, personal and occupational characteristics of those involved in the different functional areas in professional accounting firms are not necessarily homogeneous.[84]

However, the results of other studies are either inconsistent in that the nature of the differences identified are not uniform, or reveal few if any significant variations in terms of attributes or behaviour of accountants working in separate functional disciplines within accounting and audit firms. For example, whereas Purvis and Panich (1986) found there to be a higher turnover rate for audit department staff one year after joining than for taxation department staff, the results of both Barkman *et al.* (1992) and Marxen (1996) suggest that staff in taxation departments have a higher rate of turnover than staff in audit departments, while Dalton *et al.* (1997) reported no significant differences in the turnover of managers and partners across audit, taxation and management consultancy departments.

Albrecht *et al.* (1981) found significant differences on only three of twenty seven measures of job satisfaction between accountants working in audit, small business, taxation and management consultancy sections of CPA firms. Gaertner and Ruhe (1981) found no significant differences in determinants of stress between auditors, tax practitioners and management consultants, nor were there differences between the groups in terms of a whole variety of their perceptions of their work including those relating to workload, responsibility and participation. Norris and Niebuhr (1984) found there to be similar levels of professionalisation, organizational commitment and job satisfaction across audit, taxation and management consultancy staff. Moizer and Pratt (1988) found that there was little difference in the performance evaluation practices across audit, taxation, consultancy and general practice in six UK offices of four accounting and audit firms. Maupin (1993) observed that there was no discrepancy between person-centred and situation-centred explanations given by audit, management services and tax staff for the scarcity of women partners. When comparing personality types across functional area, Schloemer and Schloemer (1997) found no significant differences between audit, tax and consulting staff.

---

[84] p.26.

Hood and Koberg (1991) studied the extent to which different organizational cultural dimensions of bureaucracy, innovation and supportiveness exist within the auditing, taxation and management consultancy departments of large accounting and auditing firms. They found no significant differences across any of the cultural dimensions nor did they find any differences when they investigated measures of the creativity of personnel within these departments. In their UK study, Anderson-Gough *et al.* (1998) identified differences in the type of socialisation processes between different functional specialisms but did not find that these gave rise to differing conceptions of the role of the professional accountant. They also concluded that the differences in the sub-cultures which did exist were, at least for the two firms which they studied, less important than differences in organizational structure between the firms. They suggested that:

> It is likely that a trainee could move divisions within a firm and still 'fit in' much more easily than s/he could move between firms.[85,86]

These conflicting research results leave open the question of whether research results in the human resource management field can be generalised across all functions within an accounting and audit firm. Nor is it clear whether in future years there will be convergence across different functional disciplines, which would have significant benefits for human resource managers seeking to promote unified personnel practices within a single corporate and organizational culture: or whether increasing diversity between functional groups will force the adoption of separate human resource policies within the firms. Here there are competing forces at work. On the one hand as the lines of demarcation between specialist disciplines become much less rigid, as for example in the blurring of the distinction between audit and assurance services and consulting[87] convergence in terms of personnel and work practice is likely to occur. This will be more pronounced if the firms develop an organizational structure in which internal profit centres reflect the provision of an array of services across groupings by type of client, for example industry groupings, public sector rather than across and within the traditional

---

[85] p.123.

[86] Hood and Koberg (1991) too suggested that the culture of each individual firm dominated and suppressed any sub-cultures within different departments of that firm.

[87] See p.16 above.

groupings of audit, tax and consultancy.[88] On the other hand the divergent rates of growth across the range of services provided[89] and the increasing need for particular specialist skills and expertise beyond that which can be achieved by retraining personnel, are likely to accentuate differences between functional groups and, in turn, call for greater flexibility in human resource management practice within accounting and audit firms.

In this review we have focused primarily on those studies carried out by researchers within the accounting field which have used external auditors as subjects. These are the studies listed in the Appendix and it is a review and appraisal of these studies which forms the bulk of Chapter 4. The decision to concentrate on these studies and thereby, for the most, part only to input indirectly the results of research using accountants, more broadly defined, as subjects and of studies which have surveyed accountants other than auditors is essentially a pragmatic one, in that the advantages gained from directly incorporating a very great number of further studies into the ambit of this monograph are likely to be marginal in terms of the additional light that they shed. Indeed such an endeavour might well be counter-productive in terms of loss of direction and clarity of exposition. However, the reader who wishes to explore further in this field is directed to the Bibliography which includes more than one hundred and fifty relevant studies in addition to the ninety-six detailed in the Appendix, and distinguishes between three categories of study: those where it is known that the sample contains auditors but separate results are not reported across functional group; those where it is unclear whether the sample does or does not include auditors (although in the great majority of cases it is likely that it does); and those studies of accountants in general in which the sampling frame has been extended beyond accounting and audit firms.

---

88 Jeppesen (1998, pp.535-6).

89 Elliott (1998, p.1) characterises financial statement audit as 'no longer a growth industry'.

4 Research Findings

Introduction

Appropriately organizing and categorising the various studies which provide the base material for this review has not been an easy task. As discussed in Chapter 3, the majority of the studies have used variants of multiple regression as their primary methodology and, in circumstances where the nature and direction of causality between the various constructs being tested is problematic, it is difficult to impose an order and structure to the review which is both logical and does not involve frequent repetition. We have attempted to overcome the difficulties by setting out the findings of the studies under a number of headings which we see as encapsulating the main themes which have been of interest to researchers. Inevitably these classifications are themselves both artificial and indistinct within the interrelated and interlocking gaia representing the experience and practice of the world of work in accounting and audit firms. More prosaically, the nature of the studies themselves and the manner in which they report their significant findings make it difficult to allocate them unambiguously to one theme alone, whereas to rehearse again their methodology and motivation and to redefine the relevant variables under each heading to which they relate is likely to be both repetitious and unhelpful. To an extent these problems are intractable, but we have endeavoured to minimise this duplication of material as far as possible consistent with maintaining the clarity and flow of the individual sections.

One important theme which we have not accorded a separate heading is that of gender. Gender related issues have assumed a high degree of significance in human resource management in accounting and audit firms as recruitment patterns have shifted from being almost entirely male dominated to the present situation where almost as many females are recruited as males.[90] In recent years there has developed a significant and

[90] This situation has held for rather longer in the USA. Lehman (1992) reported that by 1980 between 35% and 50% of all new employees in public accounting were women.

rapidly growing body of what might be generically termed gender based research in accounting and auditing (Hooks, 1992; Fogarty, 1997). This research has *inter alia* highlighted the relatively low proportion of women in senior positions in accounting and audit firms, and the obstacles which confront women in advancing to senior positions within these entities with their pronounced masculine culture.[91] We have not sought to identify gender as a separate theme, in part because there have been few studies which have focused directly on gender issues as they relate to auditors alone, but primarily because so many studies include gender as a control variable that their findings, where significant, are more easily outlined within the separate theme headings under which each study is reported. We have, however, sought to draw together these findings and to highlight the importance of further gender-related research work in Chapter 5.[92]

4.1 Personality and Needs

Personality

In the UK, at least, public images of accountancy and of accountants focus on aspects of care, caution, calculative accuracy rather than on creativity, innovation, risk taking. At one end of the spectrum accountants may be perceived as possessing high ethical standards, imbued with a legacy of Victorian moral values of independence and probity, all in all worthy professional people. At the other end they may be cruelly lampooned, as in the Monty Python caricature, for their supposed lack of character.[93] Perhaps somewhere in the middle, and rather closer to perceptions in

---

[91] See for example Pillsbury *et al.* (1989), Boyer (1995).

[92] Issues of ethnicity and race as they impact accounting and audit firms too have been the subject of growing research attention particularly in North America. Studies such as those of Collins (1988), Mitchell and Flintell (1990), Hammond and Streeter (1994), Hammond (1997) and Hammond and Paige (1999) have emphasised racial barriers to entry and promotion within the accounting profession, although a study by Almer *et al.* (1998) suggested that perceptions as to the likely career progress and turnover of hypothetical recruits to CPA firms were not influenced by racial factors.

[93] In this television sketch, an individual seeking to determine an appropriate employment path is advised by a 'Vocational Guidance Counsellor' accordingly: 'our experts describe you as an appallingly dull fellow, unimaginative, timid, lacking in initiative, spineless, easily dominated...Whereas in most professions these would be considerable drawbacks, in Accountancy they are a positive boon.' (quoted in Bougen, 1994).

North America, lies the image conjured up by the popular use of the term 'beancounter' to describe the work of accountants.[94] Whether these perceptions reflect the reality of either the work or the personality of accountants is of course open to question,[95] but there is some evidence that suggests that (male) members of professional accounting bodies in the UK and Eire tend to be more socially conforming, introverted and emotionally stable than the average male. Granleese and Barrett (1993) explored the personality characteristics of male members of the ICAEW, the ICAI and the ICAS and, on the basis of their study results, drew the following picture of the stereotypical personality as that of an individual who is:

> calm, even tempered, controlled and unworried...Quiet, introspective, reserved, fond of books rather than people, he is someone who tends to plan ahead and who distrusts the impulse of the moment. He does not like excitement, takes matters of everyday life with proper seriousness and likes order in his life. He is reliable, somewhat pessimistic and he places great value on ethical standards.[96]

Arguably, the conventional image of accounting and auditing as a profession, and of accountants and auditors as individuals, does not overlap directly with the perception of individual accounting and audit firms which, since the relaxation of the rules on advertising, have striven hard to raise their profile and image in the commercial world and to the public at large. Whether this will eventually result in changes in the way accountants themselves are viewed is debatable, as in their attempts to build a brand image the firms have highlighted their role as business advisers, confidants and consultants rather than their technical skills in accounting and audit.[97]

The nature of audit and audit work means that issues of personality are of vital importance. In the relatively small group environment of most field audit teams personality clashes within the team are likely to lead to reduced efficiency and a less effective audit. At another level, the

---

[94] Two studies which survey various aspects of the public image of accountants and accountancy are those of Beard (1994) and Bougen (1994).

[95] As Bougen (1994, p.322) notes 'why a calculus consisting of partial descriptions and premised upon arbitrary allocations should become interlocked and sustained by bookkeeping images within the discourse of humour is not obvious'.

[96] p.197.

[97] For example, KPMG describes itself as 'the global advisory firm whose aim is to turn knowledge into value for the benefit of its clients, its people and its communities.' (KPMG UK Annual Report 2000, contents page).

personality traits of individual managers and partners are likely to affect significantly decisions in matters of negotiation with clients and ultimately decisions as to whether an unqualified audit report can be given. It is also the case that the interaction of personalities between auditors and their clients affects the manner in which the audit is conducted, and personal chemistry between senior employees of the client and senior members of the audit team is often cited as a reason for choice of a particular auditor.[98] Apart from their potential to affect directly audit quality, efficiency and relationships with the client, particular personality traits may be connected with a propensity to advance within the firm or to enjoy greater job satisfaction. If clear linkages between measurable personality characteristics and a successful career in audit do exist then they are likely to be of interest to those responsible for recruitment in accounting and audit firms.

The majority of the research studies that have been carried out in this area have borrowed measures of personality constructs from the psychology literature and sought to determine whether there is an interaction between different personality types and measures of work related stress, job satisfaction, turnover intentions etc. The personality characteristics which have been tested include: Type A and Type B personality, control personality, commitment disposition, challenge disposition.[99] Type A characteristics are those of an intense striving for achievement, hard driving, aggressive, competitive with a strong sense of time urgency.[100] Type B individuals are more relaxed and easy going and tend to prefer work environments that are slower paced, supportive and relationship orientated. Individuals with control characteristics tend to believe and act as if they can, through the exercise of their imagination, knowledge and skill, influence the course of events. Individuals with a commitment disposition have a tendency to become involved in whatever they are doing or encounter. Their personality characteristic is one of activeness and approach rather than passivity and avoidance. Persons with a challenge disposition believe that change rather than stability is normal

---

[98] Beattie and Fearnley (1998) surveyed 109 UK companies which had recently changed auditor. Their results suggested that although overall economic factors dominated the auditor change decision the 'chemistry' of the relationship with senior audit firm personnel was more important than the range and level of service offered. They called for further research into the dimensions of the 'chemistry' factor.

[99] See Choo (1986).

[100] See Matteson *et al.* (1984) and Ivancevich and Matteson (1988).

in working life and that change is an incentive to development rather than a threat to security.[101,102]

The main results of these studies as they relate to measures of stress, job satisfaction and turnover intentions are reported under the relevant section heading. Other findings are discussed here. Rasch and Harrell (1990) provided evidence that, for their sample at least, the presence of Type A personality characteristics was not related to the length of time an individual had been working in an accounting and audit firm. They also found evidence that female auditors were more likely to have Type A than Type B personality characteristics. Kelley and Margheim (1990) found a significant positive relationship between the audit senior having a Type A personality and the underreporting of audit time by audit juniors but found no significant associations between the personality characteristics of either audit seniors or audit juniors and the propensity of audit juniors to sign off work in the audit programme which they had not in fact completed. Fisher (2001) found that audit partners had higher Type A personality scores than other auditors.

Maupin and Lehman (1994) examined the association between a measure of personality based on gender characteristics and the likelihood of career success in the stereotypically 'masculine' public accounting firms. On the basis of a self rating questionnaire, the personality types of 461 auditors (221 males and 240 females) were classified into one of four groups: *masculine* (possessing high masculine and low feminine characteristics), *feminine* (possessing high feminine and low masculine characteristics), *androgynous* (possessing high masculine and high feminine characteristics), and *undifferentiated* (possessing low masculine and low feminine characteristics). Their results suggested that the proportion of both males and females with high masculinity scores increased with progression to higher staffing levels within the firms and that all those who reached partnership possessed either masculine or androgynous characteristics.

---

[101] It should be noted that the distinction between a personality characteristic and a work-related attitude is a fine one and that arguably both commitment disposition and challenge disposition fall into this latter category rather than being personality characteristics in their own right.

[102] Assessment of these personality characteristics is normally by means of responses to standardised questionnaires, for example the Sales Type A Personality Index - Short Form (Sales, 1969), the Locus of Control Scale (Rotter, 1966), the Organizational Commitment Scale (Porter *et al.*, 1974).

The authors counsel that the apparent need to eliminate feminine characteristics to succeed in public accounting firms may have negative consequences in that:

> the very characteristics that are undervalued, repressed or considered unimportant in partnership positions today are the ones necessary to make accounting organizations more responsive to human needs; for a sense of connectedness, community, purpose, affiliation and nurturance.[103,104]

Hull and Umansky (1997) provided a large sample of managers and partners with short cases describing the managerial styles of hypothetical managers and asked them to evaluate the perceived effectiveness of each manager. The four managerial styles chosen for experimental purposes were derived from those identified by Kroeger and Thuesen (1992). Three of the styles were perceived as dominant and 'masculine' and one empathetic and 'feminine'. The only information provided to the participants as to the sex of the hypothetical manager lay in their name, for example Janet or James.

The researchers hypothesised that men would be evaluated as more effective than women when the managerial style was masculine and less effective when the managerial style was feminine. However, their results provided little support for this hypothesis: for only one of the masculine styles were men perceived as more effective and there was no significant gender difference with respect to the feminine style.

Nor was there any evidence that male partners or female managers evaluated males or females differently although there was some evidence that male managers evaluated males who exhibited dominant, masculine styles of management more favourably than they evaluated women exhibiting such management styles.[105] One rather surprising finding was the favourable evaluations given to managers exhibiting the facilitative, empathetic, feminine management style notwithstanding the fact that it is a

---

[103] p.436.

[104] Using the same data, Maupin (1990) reported that masculine and androgynous male and female auditors gave more importance to their career than feminine or undifferentiated male and female auditors. Androgynous and feminine female auditors showed greater concern for family matters than masculine or undifferentiated auditors. Androgynous and masculine auditors placed a greater importance on the life goals of leadership and power, service to society and ethical behaviour.

[105] Female partners were excluded from the analysis because of their low representation in the usable sample.

style that rarely results in the achievement of positions of leadership.[106] This suggested to the authors that:

> Perhaps there is not, as some suggest, a need for women to adopt a masculine style so much as a need in our culture for a change of attitudes which associate the masculine image with effective leadership.[107]

Schloemer and Schloemer (1997) investigated whether the greater emphasis placed upon marketing and social skills within accounting and audit firms had resulted in the advancement of individuals with different personality traits, most notably those demonstrating greater extroversion and a willingness to engage issues on the basis of the big conceptual picture rather than a more detail-orientated approach. Their results were not uniform but did suggest that more recently promoted partners were more likely to be extrovert, in terms of dealing with an outer world of people and things rather than an inner world of ideas, than partners promoted before the new commercial orientation. There was some indication that more senior personnel were more intuitive and wide ranging in their approach to issues and problems than junior staff, but this was more clearly evidenced in non-Big Six rather than Big Six firms.

Needs

Within the general framework of research into personality characteristics, one particular focus has been on the manner in which various aspects of work related behaviour, motivation, organizational commitment, job satisfaction etc. can be linked to differences in the innate needs of individuals. Here a significant body of research has developed from the mainspring of McClelland's trichotomy of needs theory. This theory proposes that the work orientation of most individuals is motivated by their needs for *achievement*, *power* and *affiliation*. These needs are themselves seen as responses to the environment within which the individual matures, but once developed they are believed to remain relatively stable over time (McClelland and Boyatzis, 1982). Both the absolute size of each separate

---

[106] Kroeger and Thuesen (1992) suggest that an extremely low proportion of individuals exhibiting this management style reach the very top of an organization.
[107] pp.520-521.

need and its relationship to the size of the other needs are hypothesised as influencing attitudes and behaviour within the work environment.

Individuals with a large need for *achievement* are attracted to work environments in which they have personal responsibility for accomplishing difficult, but feasible, tasks and where there is clear feedback on how successful they have been in their endeavours. They enjoy situations which allow or call for innovative and novel solutions and they have a distinct orientation toward the future. Snead and Harrell (1991) argue that the nature of the work environment of public accounting firms is congruent to the achievement construct. The need to complete audit procedures within a strict time budget and to a given quality, while at the same time maintaining client co-operation within a contingent environment, provides changing and suitably challenging tasks. In addition, the nature of the performance appraisal and feedback system and the pyramidical employment structure add to the attraction of such a work environment for an achievement orientated individual.

The need for *power* is essentially a need to influence the activities and thoughts of others within the work environment, ultimately for the purpose of accomplishing group or organizational objectives, although at lower levels within an organizational hierarchy the need for power may be represented by association with powerful individuals rather than by the ability to directly influence others. Again the work environment of an accounting and audit firm with its clear hierarchical ordering and in which responsibility for the activities of others comes very early into one's career may be seen as attractive to individuals with a high need for power.

In contrast the work environment of an accounting and audit firm may be less attractive to individuals with a high need for *affiliation*. Individuals with such an orientation place a heavy emphasis on the development and maintenance of warm and friendly relationships with other people. In the early stages of a career in an accounting and audit firm the existence of a year cohort and the need to work closely together in audit teams may encourage the development of such relationships, but the competitive nature of employment in accounting and audit firms, the constant move from one assignment to another, and the relatively rapid turnover of staff are not likely to be viewed positively by individuals with such an orientation.[108]

---

[108] Dirsmith *et al.* (1997, p.10) document the competitive internal atmosphere of a public accounting firm on an anecdotal basis by reference to a training seminar for managers led by an academic consultant whose brief was to emphasise the importance of an 'I'm ok,

Comparing needs for achievement, power and affiliation with an average score derived from a validating sample used in an earlier study,[109] Street and Bishop (1991) reported that accountants in large and small public accounting firms had similar needs for achievement, moderately above the average derived from the validating sample, and similar needs for affiliation, a little below the average. Whereas employees of small firms had only an average need for power, employees of the large firms had a significantly greater than average need for power. There were also differences in terms of the hierarchical level of the employee. Managers had a much higher need for power and a much lower need for affiliation than non-managers.[110] There were no significant gender related differences.

An individual's influence-orientation has been defined in terms of the relationship between the strength of the need for power and the strength of the need for affiliation. Individuals who possess relatively large power needs in conjunction with relatively small affiliation needs are influence orientated. In their longitudinal study of new recruits to a Big Eight firm over a thirty month period, Harrell and Eickhoff (1988) identified influence orientated individuals[111] as likely to have more positive intentions to make a long term career in their Big Eight firm six months after joining and also subsequently to enjoy greater job satisfaction, display more organizational commitment and be less likely to leave the firm.

---

you're ok attitude'. The response of one manager, subsequently promoted to partner, was 'You don't understand our firm, or at least our level. Around here, it's an I'm ok, everyone else is an asshole attitude'.

[109] Stahl and Harrell (1981). In that the composition of the sample used was: 30 high school juniors, 1450 army cadets, 74 management undergraduates, 45 accounting undergraduates, 100 MBA students, 31 officer graduate students, and 11 accounting firm partners, one might perhaps question whether it was necessarily representative of the work force in its entirety.

[110] It has been argued that individuals with a high need for affiliation are less likely to make good managers in that they find it hard to make difficult decisions without worrying unduly about being disliked (McClelland and Boyatzis, 1982).

[111] For the purpose of this study an individual who displayed both an above average need for power and for whom his or her need for power was greater than their need for affiliation was categorised as influence orientated.

Summary

- **Individuals reaching senior positions within accounting and audit firms tend to possess strong masculine characteristics or a combination of strong masculine and strong feminine characteristics. Staff with strong feminine characteristics alone or without either strong feminine or strong masculine characteristics are less successful.**
- **Individuals with greater needs for power and with less need for affiliation to other individuals are more likely to make a long term career in an accounting and auditing firm. Furthermore, they are more likely to enjoy higher job satisfaction and demonstrate greater organizational commitment.**

4.2 Stress

Stress is a day to day part of the experience of life but individuals suffer stress in different ways and to a different extent. Stress may act as a spur to activity and achievement but it may also result in depression and illness. In the work place stress is normal and perhaps inevitable but reactions to stressful situations differ and excessive stress may lead to lower levels of productivity and output, absenteeism, illness, and higher levels of staff turnover. Arguably, the competitive, complex and contingent nature of the work environment within accounting and audit firms may make auditors particularly susceptible to stress.[112] In these circumstances, researchers have been interested in identifying the environmental and organizational factors that cause stress - and the closely linked condition of job-related tension - to occur. They have also sought to identify whether there are linkages between individual attributes such as age, gender and a range of personality characteristics in terms of a propensity to suffer and to cope with stress.

---

[112] The need for auditors to interact with others within the accounting and audit firm, the need to interact externally with clients in situations with the potential for conflict, together with the complexity of the modern day audit task are highlighted by Rebele and Michaels (1990) as factors likely to make auditors more susceptible than most to work place stress.

Environmental and Organizational Factors

In the behavioural literature two environmental factors are commonly identified as giving rise to stress, *role conflict* and *role ambiguity*. Role conflict is 'the simultaneous occurrence of two (or more) sets of pressures such that compliance with one would make difficult or impossible compliance with the other.'[113] Role ambiguity has been defined as the absence of the information that is necessary for persons to accomplish their role in a satisfactory manner.[114] Rizzo *et al.* (1970) devised measures of perceived role conflict and role ambiguity within organizations, based upon responses to a number of specific statements, and these measures, or variants thereof, have been widely used in research studies.

Senatra (1980) sought to identify factors that gave rise to role conflict and role ambiguity confronting audit seniors within public accounting firms. Ten factors with potential to create or diminish either role conflict or role ambiguity were identified. These were: *violations in the chain of command* - the degree to which the chain of command within the firm is by-passed; *formalisation of rules and procedures* - as regards standards of performance; work practices, policies and procedures; *emphasis on subordinate personnel development* - in terms of expectations of the manner in which seniors are expected to train and guide junior members of staff and the rewards for so doing; *tolerance of error* - whether errors are dealt with in a supportive or threatening manner; *top management receptiveness* - whether superiors are receptive to, or intolerant of, suggestions as to improved work practices etc.; *adequacy of work co-ordination* - the extent to which interrelated work activities are co-ordinated and assistance is available from other sources within the firm; *decision timeliness* - how rapidly superiors respond to problems and make decisions; *information suppression* - the extent to which both superiors and subordinates withhold relevant information; *adequacy of authority* - whether audit seniors have authority to make decisions and take responsibility; and *adequacy of professional autonomy* - the extent to which audit seniors have the freedom to exercise their own professional judgement.

Regression analysis with either role conflict or role ambiguity, measured by means of the Rizzo *et al.* scale, as the dependent variable and these ten factors as the independent variables suggested that the existence

113 Wolfe and Snoek (1962, p.103).
114 Kahn *et al.* (1964).

of role conflict was positively associated with both *violations in the chain of command* and *information suppression* and negatively associated with *formalisation of rules and procedures*. *Violations in the chain of command* was also positively associated with the presence of role ambiguity, whereas *top management receptiveness*, *decision timeliness* and *adequacy of authority* reduced role ambiguity.

The Senatra study used employees of just one large public accounting firm as subjects. Bamber *et al.* (1989) sought to establish whether there were differences in perceptions of role conflict and role ambiguity across public accounting firms, and in particular between those firms which adopted a more structured approach to the audit task and those which favoured a more open ended and flexible approach. Bamber *et al.* assessed the impact of eight organizational practices and technology characteristics. Four organizational practices were derived directly from Senatra (1980): *violations in the chain of command*; *formalisation of rules and procedures*; *adequacy of work co-ordination*; and *adequacy of authority*; and these were supplemented by *communication adequacy* - the degree to which accurate and timely information was provided when needed - and *adaptability* - the degree to which changes in circumstances were met effectively and on a timely basis. The two technology based measures were *task technology* - the extent to which tasks are characterised by unexpected and novel events - and *task analysability* - the extent to which laid down computational methods are available as compared to the need to utilise independent thought and analysis in approaching the task.

Bamber *et al.* used Kinney's (1986) dichotomy to classify each of the four firms from which participants in the study were drawn as either 'structured' or 'unstructured'. In so far as there were differences between structured and unstructured firms in respect of the measures of organizational and technological practices these were unsurprising. Audit seniors in 'structured' firms perceived their work to be characterised by greater formalisation of rules, procedures and responsibility for decision making, and that the tasks they carried out were more capable of analysis in objective, computational terms. There was evidence of a significantly higher perception of role conflict in the unstructured firms but no clear distinction between the types of firm in terms of perceptions of role ambiguity.

The impact of the eight individual organizational and technology characteristics on role conflict and role ambiguity was assessed in the structured and unstructured firms using multiple regression analysis. Role conflict in structured firms was positively influenced by *violations in the chain of command*: while in the unstructured firms it was negatively influenced by *adaptability*, *adequacy of authority* and *communication adequacy*. Role ambiguity in structured firms was positively influenced by *violations in the chain of command* and by a lack of *task analysability* and negatively influenced by *adequacy of work co-ordination* and *communication adequacy*. In unstructured firms it was negatively influenced by *communication adequacy* and *formalisation of rules and procedures*.

An earlier study (Ferris, 1977a) also pointed up the impact of the characteristics, structures and organization of individual firms in determining the environmental uncertainty confronting individual auditors. For a sample of audit juniors drawn from two firms Ferris measured perceptions of three types of work-environment uncertainty: a) the lack of information about environmental factors related to a given decision making situation, b) the inability to assign probabilities to how environmental factors are going to influence success or failure and c) not knowing the outcome of a decision in terms of how much the organization may lose if the decision is incorrect.

Overall the results indicated relatively low levels of perceived environmental uncertainty, but there were significant inter-firm differences both in terms of overall perceptions and for types b) and c) uncertainties taken individually. Ferris discussed a number of possible reasons for these differences. One was that the firm whose staff auditors had a lower perceived level of uncertainty had a client portfolio with a greater proportion of very large clients and in consequence their audit staff tended to spend longer periods of time on any one audit and did not have to adapt so frequently to new audit environments. Another possible explanation lay in the systems of employee evaluation in use in the two firms. In the firm with the lower perception of environmental uncertainty the evaluation process was two way in that audit juniors assessed the performance of their supervisors as well as being assessed themselves. Ferris considered that this provided incentives for a greater flow of information from senior to junior staff thereby reducing perceptions of uncertainty. Yet another possible explanation lay in differences between the two firms in the socialisation procedures as applicable to new staff.

Individual Factors

Individuals respond to their work environment in different ways and arguably individual characteristics play a greater part in reacting to, and coping with, stress than general environmental factors. A number of studies have sought to link personality constructs of auditors, either in isolation or in conjunction with other factors, to work related stress. These studies include those of Haskins *et al.* (1987), Rasch and Harrell (1990), Snead and Harrell (1991) and Fogarty (1995). Variables tested in these studies have included Type A and B personality,[115] interpersonal relations within work, gender, undesirable life stress, need for achievement, influence orientation, tenure in post. The results of these studies have been mixed but one consistent result has been that individuals with a high need for achievement experience less work related stress.

One study of interest was that of Senatra (1988) which focused specifically on the manner in which various potential organizational and individual stressors affected perceptions of role conflict and role ambiguity between male and female audit seniors. Unsurprisingly, for both males and females conflicting objectives enhanced perceptions of role conflict, as did the suppression of relevant information by superiors and subordinates. The presence of directives and guidelines as to job performance and excessive job and time pressures increased role conflict for males alone. For males role conflict was reduced where there was adequate work co-ordination within the firm, whereas for females it was reduced in circumstances where they had adequate authority to make decisions. For both males and females role ambiguity was reduced by the formalisation of procedures within the firm and the existence of adequate authority to make decisions, whereas adequate work co-ordination within the firm was relevant to the reduction of role ambiguity for males alone. Role ambiguity was increased for males by suppression of relevant information by superiors and subordinates, and for females by the existence of conflicting objectives, directives and guidelines within the firm.[116]

---

[115] See p.42 above for descriptions of these personality types.

[116] Fogarty (1994) found that up to the level of audit senior females exhibited more role stress (a combined measure based on role conflict, role ambiguity and role overload). However, role stress did not vary with auditor's age, marital status, rank and tenure. Fisher (2001) reports role ambiguity and role conflict to be significantly lower for partners than for other audit staff.

The three personal stressors tested were: satisfaction with time to pursue personal interests; satisfaction of family with present employment; and satisfaction with distance from relatives. For males it was time to pursue personal interests which significantly reduced perceptions of role conflict, whereas for females it was satisfaction of family with present employment which was important. Family satisfaction reduced role ambiguity for both males and females, and female role ambiguity was also reduced by satisfaction with distance from relatives. Overall, the personal stressors appeared to be slightly more important as factors underlying role stress for females than for males.

Job-Related Tension

Matteson and Ivancevich (1982) define job-related tension as an employee's physiological or psychological response to an external event, the stressor. Stressors can arise from a number of sources: the physical environment, the individual, the work group, the organization (Rebele *et al.*, 1996). Job-related tension is associated with symptoms of worrying, illness and irritable behaviour (House and Rizzo, 1972). Senatra (1980) modelled job-related tension as an outcome of both role conflict and role ambiguity and found that only role conflict was a significant factor leading to job-related tension. Senatra (1988) also found that role conflict significantly contributed to job-related tension and that, when disaggregated according to gender, role ambiguity contributed to female, but not male, job related tension. Rebele and Michaels (1990) reported that role conflict and perception of uncertainty in the work environment had a significant and positive effect on job-related tension, but again found that role ambiguity had little impact. These results held irrespective of the seniority within the organization of the respondent or their perceived need for achievement. Choo (1986) found job-related tension to be greater for those with a Type A personality and reduced by an internally orientated locus of control, professional commitment and the extent to which the job is regarded as challenging.

Rebele *et al.* (1996) assessed the variation in role conflict, role ambiguity and job-related tension over Super's (1957) career stages of exploration, establishment, maintenance and disengagement. At the exploration stage the main aim of an individual is to find an occupation in which he or she is comfortable and which will give them the opportunity to succeed. The establishment stage denotes settling on a particular occupation and the attempt to establish a secure position within the organization. The preservation of position, status and performance are the main concerns of an individual in the maintenance stage, whereas the disengagement stage is characterised by the transition from work to retirement. Rebele *et al.* (1996) found that for auditors role conflict was significantly higher at the exploration stage than at the establishment stage. Perceptions of role ambiguity and job-related tension were significantly higher in the exploration stage than in the maintenance and disengagement stages, whereas role ambiguity was significantly lower in the disengagement stage than when an individual was settling on his or her chosen career and establishing a position within the organization.

Although it may be questioned whether the nature of career development and staffing patterns within large accounting and audit firms is congruent with the model developed by Super,[117] the evidence that it is at the early stages of an auditor's career that job-related tension is at its highest prompted Rebele *et al.* to support the suggestion of Elliott (1991) that efforts should be made to provide junior auditors with more challenging assignments at an earlier stage in their career.

Summary

- **Auditors are more likely to perceive themselves as attempting to reconcile irreconcilable objectives, for example ensuring adequacy of audit testing within a restricted time budget, in circumstances where the laid down command structure within the firm is by-passed or violated and where they perceive that relevant information is being withheld by more senior personnel in the firm. Role conflict is reduced when rules and procedures as to work practices and policies in the firm are formalised.**

---

[117] In that the employment structure of accounting and audit firms *de facto* rarely offers permanent employment to professional staff below the partner level, it is arguable that the maintenance stage is inapplicable below this level. The average age of the sub-samples in the exploration, establishment, maintenance and disengagement stages were 25, 26, 30 and 41 years respectively which might also be seen as indicative of the difficulties entailed in attempting to force this model onto the particular employment structure of accounting and audit firms.

- **Auditors are more likely to display uncertainty as to their appropriate role when the command structure within the firm is by-passed or violated. They are less likely to be uncertain of their role when superior personnel are receptive to suggestions for improved work practice and respond rapidly to problems put to them. Perceived role ambiguity is also reduced when the individual has the authority to take decisions and exercise responsibility.**
- **In those firms perceived as having a more structured approach to the audit task, role conflict is greater when the chain of command is by-passed or ignored. In firms perceived as having a more flexible audit methodology, role conflict is reduced by adaptability within the organization to changing circumstances, the ability of the auditor to take decisions and exercise responsibility, and the extent to which the auditor is provided with adequate information on a timely basis.**
- **In more structured firms role ambiguity is greater when the chain of command is by-passed or violated and when there are no set procedures for carrying out particular tasks.**
- **Auditors with a high need for achievement tend to suffer less work related stress.**
- **Role conflict contributes to job-related tension for male and female auditors. Role ambiguity contributes to job-related tension for female auditors alone.**

4.3 Socialisation and Feedback

Within the human resource management literature, socialisation refers to the manner in which employees learn the attitudes and behaviours necessary in order to accomplish their role within an organization.[118] In part this is a function of formal training but traditionally auditors have gained many of their skills from working on assignments and learning directly and indirectly from their colleagues. Although the extent and nature of formal in-house training for purposes other than the passing of professional examinations has increased significantly in recent years, much of the acculturation and acquisition of specific skills of an auditor still

[118] For a more general review of the literature on professional and organizational socialisation with particular reference to the accounting profession see Anderson-Gough *et al.* (1998).

comes from 'on the job' training. In this context, Morrison (1993a) carried out a systematic study of the information seeking processes of newly recruited audit trainees, identifying which types of information were gained indirectly by monitoring and observation and which directly by enquiry. The results suggested that information about role demands and expectations, appropriate behaviours and attitudes (both within work and outside), and performance feedback was gained indirectly, whereas technical information was more likely to be sought by means of direct inquiry.

Morrison (1993a) speculates that new staff may prefer the use of monitoring and observation rather than direct inquiry so as to avoid costs associated with looking unsure, incompetent or annoying the potential information provider. In terms of the source of information there was a difference between information as to expected attitudes at work and outside, information which would be sought from experienced peers, and technical information which, together with information as to role and performance, would be obtained from supervisors. There were changes in the patterns of information gathering measured at points two weeks, three months and six months after joining the firm. *Inter alia* these included a stronger focus on performance feedback the longer the length of employment, and a change in the likelihood of obtaining information by direct inquiry as compared with consulting documentation. However, differences in methods of information seeking appeared to explain little of the variance in subjects' job satisfaction, job performance or intention to leave the firm.

Morrison (1993b) utilised this data to assess the influence of the frequency of newcomers' information seeking activities on various measures of task mastery, role clarity, acculturation and social integration two weeks, three months and six months after joining the firm. The results suggested a number of significant influences, for example task mastery was positively related to the frequency with which performance feedback was sought at each of the three points in time and to the obtaining of technical information from the immediate supervisor. Unexpectedly, task mastery was negatively related to the extent to which information was sought from peers six months after joining - a suggested explanation being that self awareness of their lack of competence led to a greater search for information. In general, although a number of statistically significant effects were identified the explained variances were relatively small and the author concluded that other factors, for example formal training courses and mentoring, played an important part in the socialisation process.

The quality of communications within the accounting and audit firm was examined more directly by Belkaoui and Picur (1987) who sought the opinions of audit seniors and managers about five information sources: the formal organization or 'the firm', immediate supervisor, co-workers, the task, and personal feelings and ideas. They focused in particular on the amount of information each source provided relating to job requirements (or referent information), the amount of information each source provided about how well the senior or manager met the job requirements (or feedback information), and the perceived reliability of each source of information. They found that the immediate supervisor was the primary source for reliable referent and feedback information, which prompted the authors to suggest that audit firms should develop the communication skills of supervisory staff through structured training programmes. In contrast to what the authors perceived as the customary image of 'the firm' as at the heart of the philosophical direction and orientation of the organization, an image consistently portrayed in training documentation and procedural manuals, the formal organization was seen by both seniors and managers as a relatively unimportant information source.

Anderson-Gough *et al.* (1998, 2001) conducted an extensive interview-based examination of the process of professional socialisation within regional offices of two Big Six UK firms. The three specific theses investigated and reported in their 1998 study were:

1. Socialisation processes focus not only upon examination performance, but also on presentation to clients and the ability to integrate with social norms of peers, managers and partners.
2. The socialisation of trainees is into organizational culture first, and professional culture second.
3. Socialisation processes vary between functional specialisms (or divisions) and give rise to differing conceptions of the role of the professional accountant.

They concluded that their first thesis was justifiable: indeed, presentation to clients and integration with peers and superiors were the centrality of the socialisation process. Examination performance was instrumental in that it was necessary to continue training and to achieve a qualification, but in itself did not denote achievement of a professional identity.

In respect to the second thesis their conclusions were less clear cut, in part because, as their subjects' notions of the profession and the meaning of professionalism were largely negotiated by the organization for which they worked, it was difficult to disentangle organizational and professional socialisation. One insight that they offered was that trainees identified much more strongly with a sense of their own career than either with the organization or the profession, although there was some evidence of enhanced organizational commitment for trainees approaching qualification.

Their third thesis they found to be false, in the sense that although there were differences in the socialisation process across functional specialisms these did not impact upon the pervasive understanding of professionalism in terms of particular modes and facets of behaviour, most notably appearance, manner and conduct.

Anderson-Gough *et al.* (2001) examined the specific issue of time management within the context of the professional socialisation of auditors. They noted how the commitment to work (including an expectation of overtime) and study for examinations curtailed leisure time but also reported that trainees perceived it as important to attend both formal and informal work orientated social events. Their interviews suggested that the practice of underreporting of overtime hours worked was widespread at both junior and senior levels, its incidence being dependent upon budgetary pressures and also on perceptions as to how to 'confer a positive impression'[119] within the firm.

Summary

- **Newly recruited auditors obtain information about role demands and expectations, appropriate behaviours and attitudes and performance feedback indirectly from peers and from other members of the firm. In contrast, they are more likely to obtain technical information by means of direct enquiry of immediate supervisors.**

---

[119] p.115

- **The extent to which newly recruited auditors engage in information seeking activities does not appear to have a very significant impact on the overall socialisation process.**
- **Appearance, manner and conduct, presentation to clients and integration with peers and superiors are important to the socialisation process.**
- **As auditors became more senior, immediate superiors appear to become a more important source for information as to job requirements and feedback as to how well the individual is meeting those requirements.**
- **Formal documentation, for example internal procedural manuals, is perceived by both seniors and managers as a relatively unimportant information source.**

4.4 Career Development

A key aspect of personnel selection policy is to seek to recruit those who are likely to be successful in their chosen career and identification of factors which are associated with successful career development is of interest to both recruiters and researcher alike.[120] One focus of research interest has been on links between the extent and nature of prior educational experience and successful career development. As we have seen,[121] in the UK recruitment into the large accounting and audit firms switched in a relatively short space of time from being predominantly non-graduate to an almost entirely graduate intake. However, the proportion of entrants into the profession with higher degrees is still low. In the USA where there has been a rather longer tradition of graduate intake (and predominantly graduates with degrees in accounting or business related subjects) there has also been a greater proportion of entrants into the accounting and audit firms who possess higher degrees (typically MBAs or accounting Masters). Wright (1988) notes that between 1973 and 1983 approximately 18% of the entrants into public accounting firms possessed MBA degrees.

A study by Ross and Ferris (1981) was based on three different samples of juniors and seniors in two different firms, and used as proxies for

---

[120] See Charnes *et al.* (1990) for exposition and discussion of an optimal hiring model applicable to auditors.

[121] See p.11 above.

successful career development and both salary levels and supervisors' perceptions of the likelihood of subjects attaining partnership. The results were not uniform but suggested that salary progression was positively influenced by the possession of a graduate degree, whereas perceptions of progression to partnership were influenced by a variety of different factors across the samples including the possession of a degree, the quality of school (university) attended, attitudinal and motivational characteristics as well as physical attributes such as height and perceived physical attractiveness. For one of the three samples possession of a Masters degree had a negative impact on perceptions of likely progression to partnership.

Ferris (1982a) analysed the influence of type of degree, academic grades achieved, and a quality rating of the institution at which the degree was achieved on initial and subsequent salary levels for a random sample of staff level auditors drawn from one large public accounting firm. Whereas at least 55% of the variation in initial salary was attributable to these educational factors their influence waned quite sharply as individuals progressed up the organizational hierarchy and by the time senior level was reached they were insignificant as a determinant of salary.

Siegel (1987) found that auditors possessing a Masters degree were promoted to senior and then to manager at a significantly faster rate than those who only possessed a first degree. Similarly, Siegel and Rigsby (1988) found that rates of promotion to senior and to manager were faster for those auditors who had benefited from an internship (work experience in a public accounting firm while still at university). Siegel *et al.* (1992) extended these studies and again concluded that, whereas either the possession of a Masters degree or internship experience was associated with accelerated promotion, auditors with just a Bachelors degree took significantly longer to achieve advancement within their firm.

However, Wright (1988) found that measured in terms of salary progression or more rapid promotional advancement the advantages of possessing a MBA degree were only marginal, although MBAs from highly rated schools did receive rather more rapid promotion to manager. Whereas the Siegel (1987) and Wright (1988) studies essentially compared sub-samples of those who achieved promotion, Spiceland *et al.* (1992) utilised survival analysis[122] (a technique borrowed from the medical literature) so as to compensate for the fact that differing proportions of the original samples might achieve promotion. This analysis suggested that the

---

122 See Cox and Oakes (1984).

median times for promotion to both senior and manager were significantly less for those entering into their career with an MBA or Masters degree compared to those entering with a Bachelors degree alone.[123]

Siegel *et al.* (1991) focused on the issue of whether prior study at a professional school of accounting and on an accredited or non-accredited accounting programme appeared to affect speed of promotion. Their results suggested that study at a professional school of accounting was associated with significantly faster promotion to both senior and manager. More recently studies in the Netherlands (Meuwissen, 1998) and the USA (Almer *et al.*, 1998) report a connection between proxies for the quality of education and actual advancement,[124] or the perceived likelihood of advancement,[125] within accounting and audit firms.

In the UK context, there has been little published research on the link between prior educational experience and subsequent career achievement. What research there has been has examined the link between factors such as 'A' level scores, degree classification, the possession of a relevant degree, possession of a degree from an 'old' as opposed to 'new' University (or from Oxford and Cambridge as compared to other Universities) on success rates in the professional examinations of the ICAEW. Here rigorous analysis is complicated by the problems of tracking cohorts through a non-uniform qualification process but there does appear to be quite strong evidence that some, but not all, of these factors are associated with differential pass rates in the professional examinations.[126]

A number of surveys have identified the relatively low proportion of females in the more senior positions within accounting and audit firms (for example, Pillsbury *et al.*, 1989). On occasion allegations of discrimination against women in the large accounting and audit firms have become headline news as in the case of *Hopkins v Price Waterhouse.*[127] Anderson

---

[123] Alford *et al.* (1990) and Bhamornsiri and Guinn (1991) both reported that the proportion of individuals possessing a postgraduate degree admitted to partnership or its equivalent was higher in consultancy and taxation than in audit. Bhamornsiri and Guinn (1991) found some evidence that audit partners did not consider postgraduate education to be an important factor in promotion decisions.

[124] Meuwissen (1998).

[125] Almer *et al.* (1998).

[126] Preliminary work by Stark and Walker (1998) suggests that A level performance, university degree grade, possession of a relevant degree, and level of numeracy all positively influence the likelihood of passing the ICAEW examinations in a timely fashion, whereas female status and age negatively affect this likelihood.

[127] *Hopkins v Price Waterhouse* 57 US LW 4469 (US Supreme Court 1989).

et al. (1994) attempted to throw further light on perceptions within the large accounting and audit firms of factors affecting the likelihood of successful career advancement. They administered a case study to auditors with, on average, five years experience for the purpose of testing the effect of gender, family circumstances and personal appearance on perceptions of the likelihood of promotion to partnership of the hypothetical audit seniors identified in the case study. Their results suggested that female auditors were perceived as less likely to achieve partnership, that single auditors were more likely to achieve partnership and that the interaction between family circumstances and gender was significant for females (which the authors argue is consistent with a scenario whereby family responsibilities are seen as a barrier to the future promotion of women). Furthermore, personal attractiveness was also perceived as likely to have a positive effect on the likelihood of achieving partnership, although this result held irrespective of gender. The authors conclude that their study reports evidence of gender, appearance and family structure bias in public accounting firms, and they suggest that the consistent results across the firms represented in their sample is indicative of perceptions of bias embedded within the organizational culture of large accounting and audit firms.[128]

In a similar study to that of Anderson *et al.* (1994), Lowe *et al.* (2001) used a hypothetical case study to examine perceptions as to the influence of gender, ethnicity (Asian, Hispanic, non-ethnic) and other factors (aggressive or quiet demeanour; individual ability; size of office etc.) on the career progression of audit seniors. The results suggested that females were more likely to be promoted to partner level in a large office than in a small office; that Asians were more likely to be promoted than either Hispanics or the non-ethnic group; an aggressive demeanour was beneficial to the career prospects for the non-ethnics and for males; and that individuals possessing high analytical skills were seen as more likely to achieve rapid career progress.

Other gender related studies[129] have highlighted the adverse effect of childbirth and child-rearing responsibilities, the excessive self-sacrifice

---

[128] In contrast, Almer *et al.* (1998) using similar methodology, but focusing upon hypothetical recruits rather than on audit seniors, found no evidence that gender or family circumstances were seen as likely to influence career progression.

[129] Pillsbury *et al.* (1989) and Fogarty (1997) summarise and review many of the studies which focus on gender issues as applicable to accountants more widely as well as to auditors.

made by, and required of, female staff, and the lack of adequate retention programmes on the career progression of women in accounting and audit firms. Some have called for further research to investigate whether more overt discriminatory practices, for example less challenging work assignments, differential performance criteria and tokenism, act to limit the opportunities for women to be promoted within the male stereotypical culture of accounting and audit firms.[130]

There has been relatively little research carried out in the UK on gender issues as they affect auditors[131] although there have been a number of historical studies charting the change in employment patterns and the attitude to women within the profession and in the wider world of accounting.[132]

Summary

- **In the USA a far greater proportion of entrants into accounting and audit firms possess a higher degree than is the situation in the UK.**
- **Auditors possessing a Masters degree, or having benefited from work experience with a public accounting firm in the course of their studies, are likely to be promoted to senior and manager more rapidly than those only possessing a first degree.**
- **Auditors perceive that females and unmarried auditors are less likely to achieve partnership. Personal attractiveness is seen as enhancing the chances of achieving partnership irrespective of gender.**

---

[130] For example Street *et al.* (1993).

[131] Moizer and Pratt (1988) found some evidence of gender differences in terms of self perceptions of effectiveness in helping their firm to achieve its goals, with males expressing greater confidence in their abilities in this role, and on some dimensions of the perceived relationship between effort and work values.

[132] For example, Kirkham (1992), Lehman (1992), Kirkham and Loft (1993).

4.5 Leadership and Mentoring

Leadership

Much of the drive and ambition which led to the early growth of what are now the great multinational accounting and audit firms came from their eponymous founders and leaders. Throughout this century the differing character and styles of senior partners within these firms has been important in determining their culture, outlook and success. Although the partnership form of structure might appear to lead to greater democracy in decision making, in reality senior partners frequently commanded great authority within the firms. For example, the merger talks between Price Waterhouse and W.B. Peat in 1921 collapsed because of the refusal of the then senior partner of Price Waterhouse to countenance the merger, although the majority of his partners supported it.[133] In recent years, as the large partnerships have evolved more formal management and decision making structures,[134] the role of the senior partner may have subtly shifted - although no doubt individual personality characteristics still play a large part in determining management style and leadership behaviour.[135] The *contretemps* over the election of a world-wide leader for Arthur Andersen[136] illustrated the importance that is attached within the firms to this post and also the differences that can arise between the more traditional accounting and auditing partners and those whose background is in management consultancy.

As leadership, whether commercial, industrial, military, political or in many other spheres, is critical to so much of human endeavour there is, not surprisingly, a voluminous research literature devoted to aspects of what constitutes appropriate and effective leadership.[137] Any attempt to distil and encapsulate this vast field of study is far beyond the scope of this monograph, but one aspect which can be highlighted is the shift from a

---

[133] Jones (1995, p.142).

[134] For example, KPMG UK now has a nineteen member Board chaired by the senior partner. Within the Board is a six-partner Executive chaired by the chief operating officer. The Executive is responsible for the operational management of the UK firm and reports to the Board (KPMG UK Annual Report 1998, p.16).

[135] See Stevens (1991) for an account which focuses on the personality characteristics and style of leading figures in the Big Eight firms at the time of the mergers, consummated and unconsummated, which led to the formation of the Big Six.

[136] *Accountancy*, July 1997, p.20 and *Accountancy*, August 1997, p.16.

[137] See Bass (1990) for a review of this literature.

normative approach, an early example of which is of course Machiavelli's handbook for effective political leadership, toward an approach which focuses on the contingent nature of leadership. As Michaelson (1973) noted: 'The primary question of research in leadership has shifted from 'what is the best kind of leadership' to 'what kind of leadership works best in what kind of situation.''[138] A second feature was the development in the 1950s and 1960s of research focusing on two particular attributes of leadership: one the manner in which leaders treat their subordinates in terms of consideration for their needs and motivation, the other the way in which leaders seek to organize and structure the tasks which their subordinates are expected to carry out.[139] This work has informed many of the studies which are relevant to accounting and audit firms. These studies, which have in the main focused on the leadership of field audit teams by audit seniors, have sought to provide input to the development of training programmes which encourage supervisory staff to adopt leadership styles that will improve the satisfaction, motivation and performance of junior staff (Pratt and Jiambalvo, 1982).

Pratt and Jiambalvo (1981, 1982) and Jiambalvo and Pratt (1982) reported the results of a questionnaire study based on thirty six field audit teams across the offices of four Big Eight firms in one US city. Pratt and Jiambalvo (1981) studied the importance of various attributes of leadership of senior field auditors by relating them to *inter alia* audit managers' perceptions of the effectiveness of the audit team performance, and also to measures of the satisfaction, motivation and quality of interpersonal relations of the audit field assistants.

The results showed that a number of leadership characteristics were positively associated with audit managers' perceptions of more effective audit team performance. These characteristics included: showing consideration to the personal needs of subordinates, allowing staff innovation, giving frequent positive reinforcement, providing infrequent negative reinforcement, offering complete and timely feedback, placing greater reliance on time budgets, and minimising the number of separate audit tasks each assistant has to carry out. These characteristics, other than those relating to the use of time budgets and the limitation of the number of audit tasks, were also positively related to the satisfaction, motivation and quality of interpersonal relations of the field assistants.

---

[138] p.226.

[139] For a review of this research see Yukl (1989).

A number of other characteristics - the extent to which the audit senior made the subordinate feel an important member of the audit team; the extent to which the audit senior assigned challenging tasks and offered encouragement; and the extent to which the audit senior encouraged and was receptive to questions - had no direct effect on perceptions of audit effectiveness, but were related to some or all of the measures of audit assistant contentment and enthusiasm. Characteristics which had relatively little effect either on audit effectiveness or on other measures included: the extent to which audit seniors attempted to orientate the subordinate to new and unfamiliar audit work (although this was correlated with staff motivation) and, perhaps surprisingly, the extent to which they engaged in task structuring.[140]

The study also threw up two linked results which raise questions as to how completely the experimental exercise was able to capture, or control for, the factors that affect the overall performance of an audit assignment, and also as to the validity of the internal performance assessments. The first was that although there was a relationship between the leadership characteristics of the audit senior and the audit manager's perception of audit team effectiveness, there was no clear association between these leadership characteristics and the audit senior's perceptions of the performance of the audit assistants. The second was that there was no evidence which supported a relationship between the performance of audit assistants as perceived by the audit senior and the overall evaluation of the audit team effectiveness.

Pratt and Jiambalvo (1982) focused on the relationship between the leadership characteristics exhibited by the audit seniors and three variables: the personality of the audit senior as measured in terms of personality dominance, the extent to which the complexity (as perceived by them) of the tasks confronting audit assistants exceeded their experience (as measured by the length of time they had been employed), and a measure of the audit assistant's intolerance of ambiguity. The results suggested that audit seniors with dominant personalities tended to engage more in task structuring and also to show a greater consideration for the personal needs of their assistants. Audit assistants who were given complex tasks, relative to their experience, tended to be working with audit

---

[140] Pratt and Jiambalvo (1982, p.371) define task structuring in the following terms: 'To the extent that the leader encourages the use of uniform procedures, defines standards of performance and lets subordinates know what is expected of them, he is engaging in structuring activities.'

seniors who showed consideration for their subordinates' personal needs, allowed them the opportunity to design their own tasks, made their audit assistants feel like important members of the audit team, assisted subordinates with the commencement of their work, and encouraged them to ask for advice from the audit senior if they ran into problems on the assigned tasks. Intolerance of ambiguity in assistants was associated with a perceived reluctance of audit seniors to allow subordinates who disliked uncertainty in their work to design their own tasks, and a tendency for the audit senior to provide more assistance at the commencement of the task.

Jiambalvo and Pratt (1982) tested the manner in which various measures of audit assistant contentment (satisfaction with supervision, the quick passage of time, task involvement) were affected by the consideration shown by the audit senior to more junior staff, the approach to task structuring taken by the audit senior, and the perception of audit task complexity. The main effects suggested that the only variable which was significantly and positively related to all three measures was, not surprisingly, the consideration shown by the audit senior. Neither structuring, nor task complexity, had direct association with either satisfaction with supervision or with the speed at which time passed, but both were significantly and positively related to a perception of greater task involvement. There were some interactive effects; for example, when the task was complex structuring reduced the perception of boredom, but when the task was simple structuring increased the boredom factor, although few of these effects were particularly strong.

Kelley and Margheim (1990) investigated further the relationship between the structuring of audit tasks and the level of consideration shown by audit seniors to their audit staff, and the propensity of audit assistants to act dysfunctionally, either in terms of claiming to have carried out work which they had not undertaken or of underreporting the actual time that their work had taken. Based on analysis of responses by audit assistants to a questionnaire, the results suggested that seniors who provided a more structured work environment tended to have fewer instances of junior staff claiming falsely to have carried out specific audit procedures, but that underreporting of audit time increased with a more structured approach to the setting of audit tasks. There was no statistically significant association between audit seniors showing more or less consideration for their junior staff and variations in either the level of audit quality reduction acts or the underreporting of audit time. However, Kelley and Margheim's results suggest that the main factor which underlies both forms of dysfunctional behaviour is time budget pressure and that leadership behaviour and personality is of relatively less importance.

In one of the few studies conducted outside the United States, Otley and Pierce (1995) pursued the same research question as Kelley and Margheim and employed similar methodology, a questionnaire approach focusing on the twin variables of acts likely to reduce audit quality and the underreporting of audit time. However, they moved up one level of seniority within audit firms in that they focused on the impact of managers' leadership style on the behaviour of audit seniors in three Big Six firms in Ireland. Their results suggested that high levels of consideration were associated with lower levels of audit quality reduction behaviour and underreporting of audit time, and this effect was stronger when a high level of consideration went together with a less structured approach. They recommended that accounting and audit firms wishing to minimise dysfunctional behaviour should direct their recruitment, promotion and training policies towards a high consideration/low structure leadership style.

They found that the perceived level of environmental uncertainty tended to have a moderating effect upon these relationships. In a relatively certain environment, the level of audit quality reduction behaviour declined as the structuring of leadership style increased, but the underreporting of audit time increased. They suggest that this arose because in a relatively certain environment and with a structured leadership style the scope for engaging in quality reduction behaviour declines and as a consequence when auditors face conflicts they have to turn to other forms of dysfunctional behaviour such as the underreporting of time. Within a highly uncertain environment a high structure-low consideration leadership style tended to lead to an increase in audit quality reduction behaviour rather than the underreporting of audit time.

Pasewark *et al.* (1994) sought to examine the effect of a finer classification of leadership attributes and used factor analysis to assess the impact of twenty three separate attributes on levels of audit junior satisfaction. The analysis suggested that these could be regrouped into four major influencing factors: a) satisfying the personal needs of audit juniors, b) defining responsibilities and communicating them to juniors, c) considering juniors' needs during the audit, and d) implementing preventative or corrective action following changes in the audit environment or below average performance levels. They also sought to investigate whether these factors impacted either on audit efficiency (in terms of the effort and cost incurred to complete the audit), and audit effectiveness (in terms of the overall quality of the audit) as assessed by audit managers, or on compliance with auditing standards and staff satisfaction as measured by audit juniors. There were significant and positive influences on audit efficiency when audit seniors were considerate to the personal needs of audit juniors, and significant and positive influences on staff satisfaction when audit seniors were considerate to the personal needs of audit juniors, defined responsibilities and communicated them clearly, and were considerate to the audit related needs of audit juniors. The authors recommend that development of these particular styles of leadership should be incorporated into accounting and audit firms' staff training programs.

Mentoring

Mentoring, whether in terms of a formalised relationship or on an informal basis is a pervasive concept within human resource management. It is of course not a new idea: as Dirsmith and Covaleski (1985) point out the term 'mentor' originates from the role of Mentor, Ulysses's trusted friend, who nurtured, protected and educated Ulysses's son during Ulysses's protracted, and arguably avoidable, absence. This is not the only example of mentoring from antiquity - perhaps even before Homer, Elijah acted as mentor to the youthful Elisha until Elisha was in a position to take over his mentor's mantle, literally and metaphorically. At a later date, Aristotle was tutor and perhaps mentor to Alexander the Great. The role of the mentor is no less important today and studies have shown that mentoring relationships can play an important part in the career development of professionals. For example, Kram (1985) found that more than 80% of professionals who became executives below the age of 40 had experienced a successful mentoring relationship.

Goss (1995) suggests that the essence of a mentoring relationship is that an individual learns and develops skills by observing and copying the behaviour, and accepting the advice of another more senior person. Dirsmith and Covaleski (1985) identify three types of mentoring relationship. The first which they term the 'true mentor-protege dyad' tends to be 'hierarchical, parental, exclusionary, elitist' while at the same time being the most wide ranging in scope and form. The second type 'the sponsor-protege dyad' is similar to the first - except that the sponsor occupies a lower rank in the organization and is therefore less well able to nurture and protect the protege. The third type is a guide-protege relationship in which the guide conveys information and advises the protege on the workings of the system and the presence of organizational pitfalls and shortcuts. In an attempt to obtain more information as to the nature of mentoring relationships within large accounting and audit firms, Dirsmith and Covaleski interviewed 110 individuals who had worked at all levels in the Big Eight firms. They found that the nature of the mentoring relationships within these firms were themselves strongly linked with the rank of the mentor and protege within the firm. They considered that the classical mentor protege relationship was only to be found at the more senior levels, in particular the role of a partner in advancing the work and interests of a manager and observing the extent to which that manager was suitable for partnership status. The relationships between audit managers and audit seniors and between audit seniors and junior audit staff possessed characteristics of the sponsor-protege and the guide-protege template. These relationships were perceived as weaker, more informational and reactive and more specifically concerned with audit assignments and tasks *per se* rather than auditing as a business and career development.

The interviews suggested that although mentor relationships, defined in the widest possible sense, were commonplace at all levels within the firms they were by no means universal and a significant proportion of individuals did not participate in such relationships either as a mentor or a protege. The benefits deriving from such relationships were seen in terms of accelerated promotion for proteges as well as enhanced familiarity with the practices and attitudes of the firm. The costs associated with such relationships included the need to show loyalty to the mentor, difficulties in dealing with individuals who did not partake in mentor activity and peer pressure from non-proteges. Furthermore, staff who did not have a mentor tended not to feel fully integrated into the firm and to suffer alienation.

In a development and extension of this study, Dirsmith *et al.* (1997) highlighted the manner in which mentor partners observed their proteges over a long period of time focusing on their performance, organizational commitment, ability to cope with increased visibility, discretion and loyalty, and their willingness to appear and behave like a partner.[141] They

[141] Dirsmith and Covaleski (1985) used the image of a mentor partner censoring a photograph showing his protege with a beard and replacing it with an older photograph in which the protege appeared clean shaven as a graphic illustration of the importance

also identified difficulties associated with male-female mentor-protege relationships as compared with those where the mentor and the protege were of the same sex, whether male or female, and suggested that the prevalence of such opposite-sex relationships may be a factor impeding the progress of women within accounting and audit firms.

This study also examined the continuation of mentoring relationships at the partner level[142] against the background of the increasing dichotomy between administrative and practitioner roles within large accounting and audit firms, and the development of the formal practice of 'management by objectives' within these firms. They found that less formal mentoring relationships still had an important role within the formal system, partners in administrative positions (for example, the managing partner of a practice office) having the role of enhancing the protege's awareness of the profit orientation and the need to meet targets within the firm.[143]

Scandura and Viator (1994) identified three aspects of the mentor-protege relationship: the provision of *social support*, for example exchanging confidences, sharing personal problems; *role modelling*, conventionally in terms of respect for the knowledge and motivation of the mentor; and *career development* whereby the mentor aids the protege, for example by giving them special assignments, advice and time. Interestingly, the only one of these aspects which was positively associated with the protege's intention to stay with the firm was that of career development. Scandura and Viator found some evidence that there was a higher level of mentoring support in the more structured auditing firms, and some suggestion that female proteges received more social support from female mentors than from male mentors.

An exploratory study by Siegel *et al.* (1995) focused on the distinction between formal mentoring programmes, in which new employees are assigned to older managers to assist their adjustment to the organizational culture and to aid their career development, and informal mentoring relationships which develop when mentors interact with, and recognise the potential of, their younger colleagues. They found that both formal and informal programmes assisted career development, itself seen as a function

---

attached to proteges conforming to norms and attitudes of behaviour if they wished to achieve partnership status.

142 Although some interviewees reported that having reached partnership the mentoring relationship which had assisted them to achieve that status ceased.

143 They suggest (p.23) that mentoring simultaneously 'promotes, transforms and constrains management by objectives' acting as an agent both to advance and confound the centralisation of power within accounting and audit firms.

of annual performance evaluations, speed of promotion, and increase in remuneration, but in different ways. The strengths of a more formal system included making the transition to a new staffing position and the learning of technical skills easier, whereas the informal system was more likely to lead to the development of personal relationships and enhance personal development (where personal development was measured in terms of self confidence, perceived ability, creativity and the ability to make decisions). There was also some suggestion that women and minority groupings may benefit more from a formalised mentoring programme than from an informal programme.

Kaplan *et al.* (1999/2000) extended prior research (Kram and Isabella, 1985) by studying peer relationships as well as mentoring relationships. Peer relationships were seen as providing benefits in terms of sharing information, discussing career strategy, and providing for emotional and psychological needs. The authors found that peer relationships, which were significantly less common than mentoring relationships, tended to supplement rather than substitute for mentoring relationships. Neither gender nor rank within the firm was significantly associated with involvement in either form of relationship but the proportion of audit staff in mentoring-only relationships increased with the size of the firm. There was no evidence that auditors with a mentor were less likely to leave the firm than auditors without a mentor. Kaplan *et al.* (2001) examined further aspects of mentoring relationships including issues as to access to mentors and perceptions of mentoring relationships by others. Although female auditors had a lower overall perception of the existence of barriers to the establishment of a mentoring relationship than male auditors, they did express greater concerns as to access and misinterpretation by others of the mentoring relationship.

In the UK context, Anderson Gough *et al.* (1998) suggest that at junior levels formal mentoring systems are difficult to operationalise successfully, in part because the exigencies of job scheduling and training make it difficult for mentor and mentee to meet on a regular basis and in part because the rapid turnover of staff means that it is difficult to ensure continuity in the mentor/mentee relationship.

Summary

- A number of leadership characteristics, for example consideration for the personal needs of subordinates, allowing staff innovation, the giving of frequent positive reinforcement, are positively associated with audit managers' perceptions of effective team performance.
- Audit seniors with dominant personalities tend to be more likely to ensure that subordinates know what is required of them within a clearly structured framework. They are also more likely to show consideration for the personal needs of their assistants.
- The satisfaction of audit assistants with their immediate work environment is positively related to the degree of consideration shown to them by the audit senior.
- When seniors provide a more structured work environment for junior staff it is less likely that audit juniors will sign off work that they have not in fact done. However, the underreporting of audit time increases in such an environment.
- There is mixed evidence as to whether a more considerate leadership style is associated with a reduction in the level of premature sign-off and other audit quality reduction acts.
- Mentor-protégé relationships exist at all levels within firms but are particularly important at higher levels within the firm. The benefits to the protégé include greater familiarity with practices, attitudes and modes of behaviour within the firm and the likelihood of accelerated promotion.
- Formal mentoring systems can be of benefit in assisting staff to make the transition to a new position and in terms of acquiring technical skills. Informal mentoring relationships are more likely to lead to greater self confidence and decision making ability in the protégé.
- At lower levels in the firm high staff turnover, and the difficulties associated with ensuring interaction between the mentor and protege, limit the effectiveness of formal mentoring relationships.

4.6 Job Satisfaction

From a human resource management viewpoint job satisfaction is essentially an intermediate construct rather than necessarily an end in itself. Arguably, from a management perspective it is job performance which is important rather than job satisfaction. However, in that there is an interaction between job satisfaction and job performance, albeit a complex one likely to be moderated by a number of variables,[144] and also an interaction between job satisfaction and staff turnover, then human resource managers are likely to be keenly interested in those factors which affect and influence job satisfaction.

Job satisfaction itself is a representation of many different aspects and facets of the world of work, and measures of job satisfaction may differ according to how successful they are in capturing these aspects and how they are interpreted and combined. Job satisfaction may relate to an innate belief in the value of the work being carried out, to a personal sense of achievement and esteem, or to working conditions or relations with colleagues, and it will almost certainly be influenced by the level of financial reward. How these factors are weighted and combined is likely to vary widely according to the attitudes, beliefs, circumstances and perceptions of individuals. The research studies carried out have tended to construct overall measures of job satisfaction as a composite of responses to questions designed to draw out perspectives on the various multi-faceted aspects of job satisfaction.[145]

In a study of audit juniors in the offices of two large public accounting firms Ferris (1977a) found that the subjects did not 'express overwhelming satisfaction with their job',[146] and that there was a negative correlation between their perceived level of uncertainty as to the environment in which they worked and their job satisfaction.[147] This was particularly manifest in circumstances where there was a perception that they were unaware of the factors taken into account when decisions were made, and where they were uncertain as to the likely outcome should the decision

---

[144] See Locke (1976) for a discussion of the issues set in the context of the wider environment of work.

[145] For example, those of Hoppock (1935) (see pp.22-23 above for further details of this measure) and Wanous and Lawler (1972).

[146] p.26.

[147] Rebele and Michaels (1990) too found that the perceived level of environmental uncertainty was negatively related to job satisfaction.

turn out to have been incorrect. However, there was some variation between subjects from the two different firms.

Benke and Rhode (1980) tested for association between a range of variables and job satisfaction for more senior staff. The variables chosen for examination were demographic (age, organizational tenure, seniority of staff level); prior educational achievement; the extent of travel demanded by the job; whether overtime worked was on a paid or unpaid basis; and the personal characteristics of self-fulfilment (in terms of work that is sufficiently challenging and appropriate to the individual's level of qualification) and sociability/ascendancy. The results suggested that older, longer serving and more senior auditors exhibited higher levels of job satisfaction than their younger and more junior counterparts.[148] Both the personal characteristics were significantly associated with job satisfaction, the greater the level of self-fulfilment the lower the job satisfaction, and individuals with higher sociability and ascendancy scores tended to be more satisfied in their jobs. The authors attributed this latter finding to the extensive interaction with colleagues and with client employees necessary in the audit environment. The other variables were not significant and the relatively low overall explanatory power of the model[149] suggested that it was failing to capture many of the factors that contributed to job satisfaction.

Harrell (1990) regressed staff auditor job satisfaction against a number of variables including initial long-term career intention, influence orientation,[150] level of education, undergraduate grade point average, a rating of the educational establishment from which the degree was obtained, need for achievement, gender, and age. Of these variables only the initial career orientation and the individual's influence orientation were positively and significantly associated with job satisfaction, none of the other variables being significant. Again the overall explanatory power of the model was extremely low.[151]

A number of studies have investigated the relationship between role ambiguity, role conflict and job satisfaction. Here the results have been mixed. Senatra (1980) found a negative relationship between role

---

[148] Fogarty (1996) also found auditors' job satisfaction to be positively associated with length of tenure (but did not vary with age, gender, marital status or rank (junior, semi-junior or senior) within the firms).

[149] The R^2 was 0.26.

[150] A composite measure based upon the difference between a measure of an individual's need for power and a measure of their need for affiliation.

[151] The R^2 was only 0.12.

ambiguity and job satisfaction, but surprisingly no significant interrelationship between role conflict and job satisfaction. Senatra (1988) found that role conflict reduced the job satisfaction of women, but not men, whereas role ambiguity reduced the job satisfaction of men, but not women. Perhaps more in line with expectations, Rebele and Michaels (1990) reported both role conflict and role ambiguity to be negatively related to job satisfaction for the subjects of their study,[152] a finding supported across the majority of Big Eight firms by Fogarty (1995) and Fisher (2001).

Snead and Harrell (1991) utilised path analysis methodology to show that, for their relatively small sample of thirty eight audit seniors, job satisfaction was directly and positively associated with influence orientation and directly and negatively influenced by work related stress. There were indirect (via work related stress) associations with non-work stress (negative) and with achievement motivation (positive). Gender had no significant effect. Using similar methodology, Rasch and Harrell (1990) reported direct positive associations between job satisfaction and both the possession of a Type A personality[153] and being influence orientated,[154] and a direct negative relationship with work related stress. There was an indirect (via work-related stress) positive relationship between an individual's need for achievement and their job satisfaction. Gender and length of tenure had no significant association with job satisfaction.[155]

The Maupin and Lehman (1994) study which focused on feminine and masculine traits suggested that the higher the level of both femininity and masculinity the greater the job satisfaction although for female subjects the femininity correlation was not significant.[156]

A study of job satisfaction over the four career stages of exploration, establishment, maintenance and disengagement[157] found job satisfaction to be significantly lower at the exploration stage relative to the other three stages, and also significantly lower in the establishment stage relative to

---

[152]These relationships were not moderated by either the staffing level of the respondent or their perceived need for achievement.

[153] See p.42 above.

[154] See p.47 above.

[155] Similarly, Fogarty (1996) found there to be no association between gender and job satisfaction.

[156] Each individual subject was scored separately for both feminine and masculine characteristics. See p.41 above and p.83 below for more detailed descriptions of this study.

[157] See p.53 above.

the maintenance and disengagement stages (Rebele *et al.*, 1996). The authors see this result as consistent with the existence of work alienation[158] at the exploration stage.

Summary

- **Factors which have been associated with enhanced job satisfaction include an initial intention to make a long term career in public accounting, a greater need for power than affiliation and a Type A (hard driving, aggressive, competitive and with a sense of time urgency) personality. Work-related stress is negatively associated with job satisfaction.**
- **Evidence as to the influence of role ambiguity and role conflict is mixed, but the majority of studies report that role conflict and role ambiguity have a negative effect on job satisfaction.**

4.7 Professional and Organizational Commitment

The great majority of auditors working for large accounting and audit firms will either possess a professional accounting qualification or be seeking to obtain one. The firms they work for are themselves hugely complex organizations seeking to portray a uniform image on a world-wide basis and making considerable demands on their staff in terms of working hours, mobility and flexibility. In these circumstances concepts of professional and organizational commitment are clearly highly relevant to auditors and those who seek to manage them. Is there a conflict between the aspects of ethical and moral integrity and public service traditionally seen as part of the professional role and the intense economic pressures within the accounting and auditing environment? To what extent do managers and partners in the large firms see themselves as part of a wider profession or is their allegiance wholly to their own firm? Does the emphasis on individual judgement and responsibility for one's actions characteristic of traditional professional values fit easily with the more integrated and managed organizations that accounting and audit firms are

[158] Work alienation being defined for this purpose as a situation in which an individual cares little about his or her work, approaches it with little energy and ambition and works primarily for extrinsic rewards.

today? Are staff with higher levels of either organizational or professional commitment more satisfied? Do they work harder and is their job performance better? How do the firms which are entrusted by the professional bodies with the task of teaching their employees to become professional people carry out that task?

In the academic literature organizational commitment has been defined as the relative strength of an individual's identification with, and involvement in, a particular organization (Porter *et al.*, 1974). Similarly, professional commitment may be considered the relative strength of an individual's identification with, and involvement in, a particular profession. Each of these commitments is characterised by a strong belief in, and acceptance of, the organization's (profession's) goals and values, a willingness to exert considerable effort on behalf of the organization (profession) and a strong desire to maintain membership in the organization (profession) (Porter *et al.*, 1974; (Aranya *et al.*, 1981)).

Professional Commitment

Research into issues relating to professional commitment relevant to accounting and auditing has been sparse, both in absolute terms and also relative to that undertaken in respect to organizational commitment. Shaub *et al.* (1993) examined the interaction between underlying ethical orientations of idealism and relativism and professional commitment. In this context, idealism refers to the extent to which an individual believes that desirable outcomes can be brought about without violating moral guidelines, whereas relativism implies the rejection of absolute moral rules to govern behaviour.[159] Perhaps not unsurprisingly, a significant positive association was found between idealism and professional commitment and a significant negative association between relativism and professional commitment. Rather more surprisingly, there was no significant association between professional commitment and the ability of subjects to identify ethical issues in a given hypothetical audit scenario.

The international nature of accounting and audit firms does raise a number of questions as to the extent to which professional and organizational commitment varies across countries and cultures. The nature and importance of professional bodies and their interaction with the

---

[159] This classification draws on the work of Forsyth (1980).

state and other economic groupings differs significantly between countries, and in many countries the Anglo-American model is an inappropriate characterisation of the nature of professionalism.[160] Organizational commitment too is likely to be culturally and historically determined, as in some countries there may be a far greater expectation on behalf of both employer and employee of a long term career within the commercial entity. Does the 'up or out' model of staff development documented earlier translate comfortably to more collective or more paternalistic societies? To date there has been little systematic research of these issues although one study, that of Jeffrey *et al.* (1996), did report a high level of professional commitment among Taiwanese auditors. This finding was at odds with their initial expectation that the more collective nature of Taiwanese society and the emphasis on loyalty to the employer organization would weaken professional commitment.

Organizational Commitment

There has been a greater volume of research into aspects of the organizational commitment of both accountants and auditors.[161] Ferris (1981) investigated association between auditors' personal characteristics (age, educational level, marital status and social background), work-related characteristics (job tenure, occupational commitment[162] and reward utility[163]) and their organizational commitment. Organizational commitment was measured by reference to two of the three factors that Porter *et al.* (1974) defined as making up organizational commitment, namely a willingness to exert considerable effort on behalf of the organization and a strong desire to maintain membership in the organization.

---

[160] See Abbott (1988) and Macdonald (1995) for further discussion of this and other issues related to professions and the nature of professionals.

[161] Gregson (1992b) identifies 23 studies of organizational commitment using accountants as subjects, although the majority of these studies included accountants in the wider fields of commerce and industry as well as those in public accounting. For a review of the measurement of organizational commitment in both accounting and non-accounting firms see Ketchand and Strawser (2001).

[162] Occupational commitment was measured by reference to whether the auditor would be happy working in another profession.

[163] In terms of pay, prospects for advancement etc.

The results suggested that the willingness to exert effort was, for audit juniors, related to job tenure and reward utility, but not to occupational commitment or to any of the personal characteristics. For audit seniors none of the variables under examination had any significant association with their willingness to exert effort. The desire to maintain membership of the organization was, for audit juniors, associated with all three work-related characteristics but again there were no significant associations with any personal characteristics. For audit seniors the desire to maintain organizational membership was significantly positively associated with occupational commitment and reward utility, and negatively associated with educational level.[164]

Shaub *et al.* (1993) hypothesised that the ethical orientations of idealism and relativism would have positive and negative effects respectively upon auditors' organizational commitment. Idealistic auditors would be happy in an environment which was committed to benefiting the users of financial statements whereas relativist auditors would be less committed to an organization that restricted individual decision making.[165] The results of the path analysis showed little direct association between idealism and organizational commitment, although there was a positive indirect association via professional commitment. There was both a direct and indirect (via professional commitment) negative association between relativism and organizational commitment. However, there was no association between the individual's level of organizational commitment and their ability to identify ethically sensitive issues.

The influence of firm structure and audit technology on the organizational commitment of its staff was investigated by Schroeder *et al.* (1992). Classifying the audit technologies of the Big Eight firms as unstructured, intermediate and structured along the lines of the Kinney (1986) model, their results suggested that managers and partners in the unstructured firms had higher levels of both organizational and professional commitment than managers and partners in firms with

---

164 Fogarty (1994) found that organizational commitment did not vary according to auditors' age, gender or rank (junior, semi-senior or senior) within the firm. Fogarty (1996) also reported no gender differences in terms of organizational commitment.

165 Although their hypotheses are to an extent borne out by the results of their study, the grounds on which these hypotheses are based are open to debate. Some would question both the commitment of accounting and audit firms to users of financial statements and the ethical values within those firms. For example, Cousins *et al.* (1998, p.9) suggest that: 'the auditing industry is pre-occupied with fees and client appeasement'.

intermediate or structured audit approaches.[166] There were, however, no significant differences in organizational or professional commitment for either audit juniors or seniors across the classification of the firms.[167] Schroeder *et al.* saw their results as consistent with the view that firms with an unstructured audit approach encourage auditors to use their professional judgement thereby fulfilling their professional expectations and leading to higher levels of organizational and professional commitment. They argue that this effect is only detectable at more senior levels within the firms, because further down the hierarchy the audit task is more mechanical in nature and there is less need for the use of professional judgement, irrespective of the audit approach taken.

The results of this study also suggested that as individuals progressed upwards through the hierarchy of accounting and audit firms their organizational commitment strengthened whereas their professional commitment did not. The authors attribute this to the realisation that loyalty to the organization rather than the profession is necessary if a successful career is to be achieved within the firm.

Gregson (1992b) reviewed issues of causal ordering in relation to job satisfaction and organizational commitment and the link to turnover intention. Essentially the question addressed was whether organizational commitment is causally antecedent to job satisfaction or whether job satisfaction is antecedent to organizational commitment. Studies conducted outside the accounting arena[168] have yielded conflicting results both in terms of the direction of the causal link and indeed whether there is any causal link. In studies involving accountants the proposed causal ordering has been inconsistent too, although all the studies have reported a significant positive relationship between the variables. Gregson sought to to throw further light on this issue by applying structural equations methodology to data derived from two earlier studies of accountants' job satisfaction, organizational commitment and turnover intention.[169] The

---

[166] Only two of the Big Eight firms, Price Waterhouse and Coopers & Lybrand, were classified as unstructured.

[167] In contrast, Fogarty (1995, 1996) reported differences in organizational commitment among audit juniors across Big Eight firms, specifically organizational commitment being higher for auditors with longer tenure. Although he did not seek to differentiate according to structure, the level of organizational commitment, and the impact of role ambiguity, role conflict and a number of job-related characteristics upon the level of organizational commitment, varied across the firms.

[168] For example, studies of nurses, mental health personnel, insurance company employees.

[169] Data was obtained from Lachman and Aranya (1986a) and Colarelli *et al.* (1987).

results suggested that modelling job satisfaction as an antecedent to organizational commitment was more successful in predicting turnover than modelling organizational commitment as an antecedent to job satisfaction.

In a study of junior auditors in one large accounting firm, Harrell (1990) utilised hierarchical regression analysis[170] to explore the extent to which the relationship between organizational commitment and job satisfaction was a reciprocal one. The results suggested that the relationship was reciprocal, a finding which the author saw as offering a logical explanation for the conflicting results presented in prior research as to which of these constructs is a determinant of the other. The existence of a reciprocal relationship was seen as having practical implications in that managers wishing to positively influence the long term career intentions of their junior level audit staff should seek out a strategy designed to simultaneously increase job satisfaction and organizational commitment. Such a strategy might encompass aspects of the work environment such as challenging assignments, a clearly defined career path, leadership opportunities etc.[171]

Potential gender differences were identified by Street *et al.* (1993) who investigated differences in the levels of organizational commitment between males and females. Males displayed significantly higher organizational commitment than females at both lower and higher levels in the organization. The authors suggest these differences may be a product of dissatisfaction with the opportunities for advancement open to women in public accounting firms.[172] This finding contrasts with that of Harrell (1990) who found no significant gender related differences in terms of organizational commitment.

Compatibility of Professional and Organizational Commitment

As noted above, it has been questioned whether professional and organizational commitment are compatible. One potential incompatibility

---

[170] See Cohen (1978).

[171] In the model there were significant associations between the auditor's educational level, undergraduate grade point average, the quality of the educational establishment attended and organizational commitment, but these only explained a small part of the variance (the R^2 was 0.14) suggesting that many other constructs influenced the organizational commitment of junior auditors.

[172] No differences were identified in respect to professional commitment.

lies in the contradistinction between the professional emphasis on the individual, individual autonomy and individual judgement and the organizational emphasis on corporate structures and hierarchical control, an adherence to formal and informal internal codes and regulations, and on uniformity of approach and presentation.[173] A linked but separate arena for potential conflict lies in the public interest orientation of professional bodies as compared with the essentially commercial imperatives of the individual firms. When confronting a decision whether to comply with a client's wishes as to a particular financial reporting issue, an individual auditor may face conflict between a desire to provide users of the financial statements with the most objective information and a desire to retain the client and thereby enhance his or her position within their firm.

Others would argue that this dichotomy is overly simplistic and fails to reflect the fact that the process of professionalisation is very largely accomplished within the firms themselves.[174] Here the argument is that the initial focus within the firms is on developing professional commitment, and that over time this melds into the development of organizational commitment as the individual aligns himself or herself more closely with the goals and objectives of their employer.[175] There is some evidence, for example Shaub *et al.* (1993), that for auditors the development of professional commitment precedes the development of organizational commitment. However, the subrogation of almost the entire responsibility for the development of professional values and attitudes to the accounting and audit firms, and in particular to the large firms, does raise questions as to whether the values being transmitted are those traditionally associated with professionalism. In this context it is interesting to note that in their study of organizational and professional socialisation within two large UK accounting and audit firms Anderson-Gough *et al.* (1998) presented an image of

> trainee socialisation offering little in terms of a sense of a distinctive 'professional' identity in the sense that it can be distinguished from the firm's

---

[173] Studies focusing on these issues include those of Gouldner (1958), Shepherd (1961), Sorensen (1967), Sorensen and Sorensen (1974).

[174] Whereas in the US, certain aspects of professionalisation, for example the focus on ethical values and judgements, may take place as part of the prior educational process, in the UK, with the possible exception of Scotland, professionalisation is almost entirely a product of the work place.

[175] See for example Wilensky (1964), Larson (1977).

organizational socialisation: being professional seems to be suggestive of norms of conduct in relation to dress, attitude and behaviour.[176]

Professionalism was essentially seen in terms of conduct and behaviour rather than identity with a professional body and that conduct and behaviour was viewed as an art of impression management for the benefit of clients.

Summary

- **Auditors with a greater belief in the existence and validity of absolute moral rules (idealists) display a greater commitment to, and involvement in, the accounting profession than those who believe that ethical considerations are essentially relative in nature.**
- **There is little direct association between auditors' level of idealism and their commitment to the goals and values of their organization, but there is a negative association between the level of relativism and organizational commitment.**
- **Managers and partners in firms with a less structured approach to audit display higher levels of organizational commitment than managers and partners in more structured firms.**
- **There is some evidence that the development of professional commitment precedes the development of organizational commitment. However, organizational commitment increases as individuals reach more senior positions within their firm whereas professional commitment does not.**
- **In the UK at least, for many junior employees professionalism and organizational commitment are virtually indistinguishable, both being couched in terms of dress, attitude and behaviour.**

4.8 Staff Turnover

The turnover or turnover intentions of professional staff within accounting and audit firms has been the subject of extensive study. A number of North

---

[176] p.91.

American studies[177] conducted from the 1960s onwards highlighted the relatively short period of time for which most accountants stayed with their first employer. The evidence was that rather more than half of new recruits to public accounting firms left within four years and that approximately 80% departed within six years. Furthermore, there was some suggestion that the average length of stay of accounting professionals in public accounting firms was shortening in the 1970s and 1980s (Earnest and Lampe, 1987). The authors of these studies suggest this high rate of turnover to be excessive and costly. For example, the office of a public accounting firm chosen for study by Bullen and Flamholtz (1985) showed an annual rate of staff turnover of 34% as compared with the partners' target rate of turnover of nearer to 20%. Earnest and Lampe (1987) reported that their discussions with partners in large accounting firms indicated that audit staff turnover was a continuing problem. These studies identified costs of such high levels of turnover in terms of recruitment expense and the need to supervise and train new recruits.[178] More indirectly, Bullen and Flamholtz identified costs consequent upon dissatisfied ex-employees joining a client or prospective client, whereas Earnest and Lampe focused on costs resultant upon decreased social integration, and the enhanced bureaucracy necessary to compensate for lack of staff familiarity with each other and with the working practices of the firm. A more recent study, Hermanson *et al.* (1995), highlighted client resistance to continual change of personnel in the audit team. The conventional view that it is necessary to keep and retain staff is echoed by Bullen and Flamholtz:

> Since owner-partners have invested and are planning future investments in human resources with the expectation of realizing a good return, it seems reasonable that owners would seek ways to protect their human capital investments.[179]

---

[177] For example, those of Ellyson and Shaw (1970), Montagna (1974), Steele (1976), Tyra (1980), Benke and Rhode (1984), Bullen and Flamholtz (1985), Earnest and Lampe (1987).

[178] In the UK, Wyman (1997) suggests that the revenue generated from student accountants during their three year training contract is hardly sufficient to cover their costs of employment and training. He notes (p.73) that 'A student on a three-year training contract, who barely covers costs during the training contract, who leaves his training firm immediately on qualification, is scarcely an attractive proposition!'.

[179] Bullen and Flamhotz (1985, p.288).

However, as has been noted before, the picture is rather more complex than this. Although, the great majority of departures from accounting and audit firms are voluntary this does disguise an underpinning employment pattern which has a high turnover rate built in. The extent to which this is a consequence of the desire of the firms for a highly competitive and flexible work force in which the prospect of status and financial rewards are available to those relatively few who successfully negotiate the path to partnership, or to which it is driven by the aspirations and perspectives of those who enter employment with accounting and audit firms, is an open one. For many the training in the accounting and audit firm is seen as an end in itself with only a limited expectation of an extended career within that firm. This is in part borne out by the significant number of accountants who resign after completion of their training (Robson *et al.*, 1996). Here perhaps there is an analogy with the medical profession in which all doctors train in hospitals but a much smaller proportion continue to remain employed by the hospital in which they trained for any significant period after qualification. More generally, Snead and Harrell (1991) contrast what they characterise as normal employment practice, in which people in organizations leave for relatively similar posts in other organizations, with the more distinctive nature of the move which accountants leaving large public practice firms make, whether it be to enter industry or commerce or to switch to the very different environment of a smaller accounting and audit firm.[180]

Although most of those who leave accounting and auditing firms do so on a voluntary basis the use of the term voluntary disguises a spectrum of situations and circumstances and for many the decision to leave is effectively dictated within this spectrum. In the large accounting and audit firms there is clear differentiation in terms of remuneration and timing of promotion from an early stage in the progress of any one entry cohort. For many the signal that partnership is unlikely to be within their grasp comes very early in their careers[181] and they adjust their perspectives accordingly. Others perhaps initially more successful, or perhaps more willing to persevere in the competitive internal structure, may be actively 'counselled out' further down the line. For many years the growth of the profession and the extent of job opportunities for qualified accountants meant that

[180] A similar point was made by Rhode *et al.* (1977) who described the turnover process as migration from the large public accounting firm work environment to other work environments.

[181] In the terminology reported by Dirsmith *et al.* (1997) those who are not 'on the bus'.

enforced (again in the strict sense of the word) departures were, in the UK at least, few and far between. However, as became clear in the early 1990s in the UK, the size of modern accounting and audit firms, and the number of trainees that they employ, means that the balance between recruitment and departures is highly vulnerable to economic downturn. In the then sharp recession the lack of alternative employment opportunities greatly reduced the number of 'voluntary' departures, and, as a consequence, the large firms were forced to lay off professional staff in a fashion unprecedented in previous adverse economic climes.

Many academic studies have sought to model either actual turnover of accountants or the turnover intentions, i.e. the likelihood of leaving within a specified time period whether it be one, three or five years. Models have been developed of intention to leave individual organizations,[182] the large firm environment,[183] the accounting profession,[184] and more general measures of turnover intentions or desire to leave 'the job'.[185] Here the term model covers a variety of types of study. Some focus primarily on associations between turnover and particular employee characteristics such as age, education, gender, personality. Others seek to delve a little more deeply into what actually causes individuals to change their jobs and endeavour to relate the statistical associations uncovered more directly to aspects of the work environment and the nature of the work conducted. Although the distinction between the two types of study is not always clear cut, and much of the research carried out bridges across the two,[186] these two research approaches may be seen as having rather different implications and orientations for those charged with responsibility for human resource management in the large accounting and audit firms. Association studies may lead to a focus on the recruitment of staff with particular characteristics - because the statistical evidence is that they are likely to stay with the firm longer. Studies of the underlying causes of

---

[182] For example, Rhode *et al.* (1976, 1977), Dillard and Ferris (1979), Senatra (1980), Aranya *et al.* (1982), Aranya and Ferris (1984), Bullen and Flamholtz (1985), McGregor *et al.* (1989), Meixner and Bline (1989), Gregson (1990a), Brierley and Turley (1995), Smith *et al.* (1995), Pasewark and Strawser (1996).

[183] For example, Rasch and Harrell (1990), Snead and Harrell (1991).

[184] For example, Meixner and Bline (1989).

[185] For example, Scandura and Viator (1994), Harrell *et al.* (1986), Senatra (1988).

[186] For example, those studies which relate job satisfaction or organizational commitment to turnover. Although some types of individual may have a greater innate propensity to enjoy job satisfaction or to demonstrate organizational commitment these characteristics are also capable of being influenced by the work environment created.

turnover may prompt action to change or modify the work environment in a manner that will persuade staff to stay longer, in particular those individuals whom the firm is anxious to retain.

Most studies encompass the turnover intentions of accountants in general. Here we report on the salient features of a number of the more recent studies which have focused on auditors *per se*. Again, unless specifically otherwise identified, all of the studies are based on US data.

The question of whether there is a clear link between turnover and prior educational level has been investigated by Siegel (1987), Wright (1988), Siegel *et al.* (1991) and Spiceland *et al.* (1992).[187] Here the evidence is mixed. Siegel (1987) and Spiceland *et al.* (1992) both found auditors with just a Bachelors degree to have higher turnover rates than those with a Masters degree. However, Wright (1988) found no such difference, although when a distinction was made as to the rating of the school from which the Masters degree was held, he did find that alumni of the higher rated schools had significantly lower turnover rates than both alumni of lower rated schools and those who did not hold a Masters degree. Siegel *et al.* (1991) found that at both senior and manager level turnover rates for auditors who had graduated from professional schools of accountancy were lower than those who had graduated from non-accredited accounting programmes. At the senior level graduates from accredited accounting programmes had significantly lower turnover rates than those from non-accredited programmes but this distinction did not hold at the manager level.

A number of studies have investigated whether there is any significant difference in turnover intention and patterns between male and female staff. Here again the evidence is mixed. In a study based on one Big Eight firm, Harrell and Eickoff (1988) found that six months after joining the firm female staff expressed a significantly lower commitment to pursuing a career within the firm than male staff, but that eighteen months after joining the firm this difference had disappeared. Fogarty (1997b) too noted that up to the level of audit senior female staff were more likely to leave. Harrell (1990) found that long term career intention did not vary according to gender. This finding was supported by the Rasch and Harrell (1990) study which showed that there was no significant difference in turnover intention within a three year time horizon for audit juniors and seniors. However, Rasch and Harrell did find that in the higher echelons of

[187] These studies are discussed in more detail on p.57-58 above.

the firm (manager and partner level) females were more likely to express an intention to leave within three years than males.[188]

Maupin and Lehman (1994) sought to explore further how gender related characteristics affected turnover patterns. Turnover was measured on the basis of whether the subjects were still employed by their firm five years after the collection of the data relating to gender, and was analysed across the gender characteristic classifications: masculine, feminine, androgynous, undifferentiated.[189] The results showed that androgynous subjects had the lowest rate of turnover followed in order by subjects with masculine characteristics, those who were undifferentiated and those with feminine characteristics. The results held irrespective of whether the subject was male or female (although for female subjects there was no difference in turnover rates for androgynous and masculine classifications). Low job satisfaction was only linked to high turnover for the undifferentiated and feminine classifications, androgynous and masculine subjects who left their firms had exhibited high job satisfaction at the time the original survey was carried out.

A survey by Hermanson *et al.* (1995) asked participants to rate the importance of a number of work environment related factors and potential changes to that environment in determining whether or not to pursue a career within the accounting and audit firm. They focused in particular on the difference between male and female auditors in the importance they assigned to particular factors. For example, female auditors placed more emphasis on child care assistance, alternative work arrangements, knowing the time at which work would end for the day, the availability of a stress management course. To the authors this is a reflection of the fact that, notwithstanding a degree of role adjustment in modern society: 'women generally still bear the majority of the household burden, they are especially challenged in balancing their personal and professional responsibilities'.[190] They suggest that firms should seek to make special work arrangements for female staff, and also that they should have more flexible working hours and a greater willingness to employ part-time staff to assist at peak periods.

---

[188] Similar findings were reported earlier by Earnest and Lampe (1982). More recently, Almer *et al.* (1998) found evidence that female auditors were more likely to leave than males and auditors with a family were more likely to leave than single auditors.
[189] For further description of these classifications see p.43 above.
[190] p.43.

A priori reasoning would suggest aspects of role conflict, role ambiguity, job satisfaction, organizational-professional conflict etc. to be inextricably linked to turnover intention and indeed the majority of the studies do identify such linkages, albeit with some exceptions.[191] The degree of the sophistication of these studies and the extent to which they seek to differentiate between direct and indirect influences on turnover intention varies. Harrell (1990) found that the only construct that directly influenced the likelihood of voluntary departure two, three and four years after joining the public accounting firm was the long term career intention of remaining in public practice as measured one year after joining. Job satisfaction and organizational commitment did not in themselves have any direct impact on actual turnover, but did have an indirect effect through their influence on long term career intentions. Rasch and Harrell (1990) found that turnover intentions were significantly, directly negatively related to the degree of influence orientation of the individual, their job satisfaction, the length of time for which they had worked for the firm and the possession of a Type A personality. Work-related stress had an indirect positive effect operating via job satisfaction, whereas the individual's need for achievement indirectly affected turnover intention, individuals with a high need for achievement being less likely to leave. Snead and Harrell (1991) found that the long-term intention of audit seniors to remain in the work environment of a large accounting firm was directly and positively influenced by their perceived level of job satisfaction and also by the hours which they were willing to work.

Studies which have sought to analyse more closely the factors which cause individuals to seek out alternative employment include those of Dillard (1976, 1979) and Earnest and Lampe (1987). These studies use variants of an expectancy theory model which links both the desirability of certain outcomes, for example, higher pay, opportunity for promotion etc. and the perception that the individual can influence these outcomes by his or her own efforts. Underlying the model is the assumption that individuals maximise utility on the basis of the trade-off between effort and the expectation of certain outcomes. If alternative job opportunities offer the potential for higher utility then the individual is likely to leave.

---

[191] For example, Senatra (1980 and 1988) found no significant relationship between turnover intention and either role conflict or role ambiguity, whereas Fogarty (1995) found that for audit juniors high levels of role conflict and role ambiguity were linked positively to turnover intention.

The Dillard (1976) study suggested that auditors intending to leave public practice to work in industry placed greater emphasis on desirable outcomes such as job security, warm interpersonal relationships, freedom on the job, promotion opportunities, a feeling of helping others: and on negative outcomes such as the undesirability of working out of town, working under pressure, working overtime, working in a formal environment, the need to show loyalty to the firm rather than the profession and the pressure to conform both inside and outside work. Earnest and Lampe (1987) employed an expectancy model which sought to compare perceived motivation in an alternative job to that in the present auditing job. Factors studied included those that the authors termed 'intrinsic rewards', for example relationships with co-workers and successful achievement of task related goals, and 'extrinsic rewards', for example remuneration, amount of leisure time, promotion, recognition. The results suggested that auditing was perceived positively in terms of certain of the intrinsic rewards, for example relationships with colleagues, but negatively in terms of the type of task performed. The further the subject had risen in the firm hierarchy the greater the perception of the value of the intrinsic rewards in the accounting and audit firm as compared with those available in alternative employment. In terms of extrinsic rewards alternative employment was seen to hold out the prospect of more leisure time and also of performance related financial rewards.[192]

Summary

- **There is some evidence that auditors who possess an undergraduate degree alone have higher turnover rates than those with a Masters degree, but there is also evidence that other factors, for example the quality of the University attended, may have a more significant effect than the level of the degree alone.**
- **At more senior staffing levels female auditors are more likely to express an intention to leave the firm within a given time frame than males. At lower levels within the firm there is less evidence of**

---

192 The Hermanson *et al.* (1995) survey suggested that changes in the day to day work environment, in particular the proper staffing of audits and the use of more realistic time budgets and deadlines, would encourage audit juniors to foresee a longer term career in their firm.

differentiation between males and females with respect to turnover intentions.

- **Turnover intentions of individuals are influenced by their long term career intention; their satisfaction with their job; the number of hours that they are prepared to work; as well as by a number of specific personality characteristics.**

4.9 Performance Appraisal

Accountability and appraisal are ever present within a large accounting and audit firm. In part this is a reflection of the nature of the work carried out and the manner in which it is budgeted and charged for. Typically, at all levels within the firm staff have to keep records of and account for every hour of their time.[193] Time sheets are normally completed on a weekly or monthly basis and each hour worked allocated to a code such as work for a client, training, studying etc. Although charges to clients are no longer mechanistically driven by multiplication of chargeable hours by the appropriate charge out rate, if indeed they ever were, nevertheless comparison between budgeted costs and actual recovery from the client is important. Not only do staff have to account for every hour that they work but they also face a pervasive and invasive system of review and formal appraisal. The review system, which is designed to ensure an appropriate quality of work and ultimately an appropriate audit opinion, means that in theory at least every aspect of work carried out is liable to detailed check, normally by someone at the next level of the hierarchy. Typically an audit junior's work would be checked by an audit senior, an audit senior's work by an audit manager and that of the manager by the engagement partner.

Although the system of review and check might appear to be almost foolproof the reality is very different. The nature of many audit engagements carried out under acute time and budget pressure is such that there is neither the energy nor the incentive to demand or engage in reperformance of the audit tasks which it is claimed have been carried out.[194] A number of studies have documented that a not insignificant

---

[193] In some firms the accountability requirement extends to units of time as small as quarter an hour. Andersen-Gough *et al.* (2001, p.113) report a perception that typically trainees and managers had to 'account for every six minutes of the day'.

[194] Asare and McDaniel (1996) suggest that the incidence of reperformance is very low even where time and budget pressures are not perceived as acute.

proportion of auditors admit to having signed off, some on a routine basis, audit tasks that they had not in fact carried out. In part this may be a reflection of the monotonous and tedious nature of certain checking procedures, procedures which may seem to have little relevance or coherence to the overall audit, in part it is no doubt a reflection of the perceived pressures at all levels to bring in assignments within budget.

There is now a corpus of research work which focuses on various aspects of review procedures within accounting and audit firms, for example how successful reviewers are in extracting messages and warning signals from working papers, whether different review approaches are more effective than others, whether familiarity between the reviewer and the reviewee aids or hinders the review process etc.[195] These studies are at a slight remove from the main theme of this monograph and are not considered in detail here.

The review mechanisms do not in themselves constitute part of the formal appraisal process, but they do feed into a system where on every assignment each person working on the audit field team is normally assessed across certain categories as to their performance on that audit. This assessment is normally the responsibility of the next person up the reporting hierarchy, juniors being assessed by seniors, seniors by managers, managers by partners. These assessments will then form an important element in six monthly or annual appraisal meetings. These meetings may be with audit managers or partners with human resource management responsibilities, or with full time human resource management personnel.[196] In that in most firms differential levels of seniority and remuneration are introduced very early into the career path of a cohort of recruits, these assessments have a key role in determining how an individual's career develops within the firm.[197]

A number of attributes have been identified as desirable characteristics of performance appraisal systems. These include: influencing employees' perceptions as to the job dimensions which their superiors regard as important;[198] assisting in motivating employees to align themselves more closely with increased work effort, improved performance and higher

---

[195] Ramsay (1994) and Asare and McDaniel (1996) are examples of such studies.

[196] See Anderson-Gough *et al.* (1998) for a description of the UK appraisal practices of two Big Six firms.

[197] Wright (1980) suggests that audit seniors' appraisal of audit juniors is the main factor determining the promotion and salary progression of the audit juniors.

[198] Kida (1984).

rewards;[199] and providing employees with feedback which they can utilise to improve their overall performance.[200] A number of research studies have sought to further our knowledge of the actual operation of performance appraisal systems and whether they do in fact possess the necessary characteristics to assist in successful human resource management.[201]

Two early studies,[202] focused on whether the appraisal criteria which audit staff believed were important were in fact those which audit partners believed to be important (accuracy), and whether the criteria which audit staff believed *were* important were those which they, the staff, thought *ought* to be important (congruence). They also tested whether there were relationships between accuracy and congruence and both staff satisfaction with the evaluation process and their overall performance.

The Maher *et al.* study, which included staff of all levels, found some differences in terms of both accuracy and congruence but these differences narrowed significantly as staff rose through the hierarchy. However, there was no clear cut relationship between accuracy or congruence and overall performance evaluation. The Jiambalvo study, which investigated the accuracy and congruence of the perceptions of audit seniors, also found significant differences. Again, however, there was little clear evidence that either agreement between senior and partner as to what was important, or congruence between audit seniors' perceptions of what should be and what was important, had significant association with either seniors' satisfaction with the evaluation process or perceptions as to their performance. The Jiambalvo study covered three separate offices of one large firm and when the data was disaggregated some office specific associations were uncovered which prompted Jiambalvo to call for further investigation of particular office effects in appraisal research.

A more recent study, Emby and Etherington (1996), found smaller differences in perceptions as to the importance of appraisal dimensions across their sample than those reported in the earlier studies. There were however significant changes in the ranking of the importance of individual dimensions as individuals became more senior within the hierarchy of their firm. Whereas 'technical skill' was seen as the most important appraisal dimension for junior auditors, at the manager level it was only ranked

---

199 Jiambalvo (1979), Jiambalvo *et al.* (1983), Kida (1984).

200 Hassell *et al.* (1992).

201 A comprehensive review of research into performance evaluation in accounting and audit firms is found in Hunt (1995).

202 Maher *et al.* (1979), Jiambalvo (1982).

fourth of the seven dimensions tested.[203] One consistent result was that the development of junior staff was lowly ranked as an appraisal dimension at all stages of an individual's career. Inter-firm differences were relatively minor and gender had no significant impact on the results.

Wright (1985) focused on whether, in carrying out their appraisals, seniors weighted key job dimensions in a manner similar to that of personnel administrators. A comparison across seventeen job dimensions showed that there were only significant differences in perceptions as to the importance of just two dimensions. Personnel administrators believed that written communication skills were more important than did seniors, whereas seniors placed greater emphasis than personnel administrators on the ability of staff to train and develop subordinates. This study was in part an extension of an earlier study, Wright (1982), which sought to determine which of four criteria were the most important in the assessment by an audit senior of the overall performance of an audit junior. The criteria chosen related to the *technical skill* of audit juniors, their *motivation level and willingness to accept responsibility*, their *communication skills* and their *ability to meet time budgets*. Presented with hypothetical information relevant to each criterion for a number of audit juniors the results showed that it was perceived technical ability which was the main driver underlying the overall performance assessment.

The finding that it is technical competence which is the most important factor in overall performance assessment was corroborated by Kida (1984).[204] In this study audit seniors and audit managers were required to provide an overall performance evaluation based on hypothetical profiles of audit seniors together with ratings across seven specific dimensions of job performance. Technical competence was found to be by far the most important dimension identified by both seniors and managers. In aggregate the study found no significant differences between the manner in which seniors and managers evaluated audit staff, but this aggregate result concealed significant differences between individual seniors and managers as to the relative importance of various dimensions. Clearly such differences could have important implications for the appraisal of individuals within the firm, notwithstanding the fact that in the aggregate the differences largely cancel each other out.

---

203 For similar results, see Bhamornsiri and Guinn (1991).

204 However, Regel and Murray (1989) suggested that 'people relations' weighed more heavily in performance appraisal than 'technical skills', although this was based on a sample of just three senior appraisers.

Wright (1980 and 1985) considered it surprising that, given the importance of the performance appraisal system within the overall human resource management profile, few accounting and audit firms adequately trained staff to carry out appraisals or observed and monitored those appraisals.[205] One study which focused on training staff, albeit junior staff, to be alert to the importance attached to various performance dimensions, was that of Regel and Murray (1989). A group of junior auditors who had received training designed to improve the accuracy and consensus of their evaluations of the relative importance of various performance dimensions, and an untrained control group were given an experimental task involving hypothetical staff profiles. Perhaps not surprisingly, the results showed that training junior auditors as to the importance attached by partners to aspects of the performance evaluation system led to a significantly better correspondence between junior auditors and partners with respect to the weights attached to different performance evaluation dimensions.

Suggestions for improvement in the manner in which appraisal is carried out were made by Wright (1985 and 1986) who advocated the use of Behaviourally Anchored Rating Scales (BARS).[206] BARS incorporate descriptions of the type of behaviour that is associated with good and poor performance rather than utilising conventional rating scales. Wright argued that many of the dimensions being assessed on then conventional rating scales were poorly specified, for example 'disciplined approach to work', 'appearance'. Furthermore, the scales themselves typically incorporated value-laden terms such as 'excellent', 'above average', 'below average' but did not define the basis on which these were to be interpreted and applied. In contrast, BARS provide examples of behaviour attributable to good, average or bad performance for each job dimension thereby allowing the rater a benchmark against which the observed behaviour can be assessed. A BARS based appraisal system is seen as reducing the likelihood of both a halo effect, when an appraiser relies on only one or two factors or a general impression as a basis for evaluating all factors, and leniency, the tendency to provide undeserved high ratings for all staff appraised. In conjunction with audit seniors and supervisors, Wright (1986) developed such a system for assessing the performance of staff auditors. This involved the identification of nine performance dimensions

[205] Wright (1980) reported that seniors in large public accounting firms received an average of only five hours of formal training on performance appraisal problems and techniques.

[206] See Dunnette and Borman (1979) for a more detailed description of BARS and their application in other employment areas.

categorised across four areas: - *technical and analytical skills:* creative; efficient and organized working papers; knowledge of accounting and auditing standards/theory; and judgement and common sense, *interpersonal skills, communication skills,* and *professional characteristics:* initiative and ambition; and maturity and confidence - together with associated examples of high, mid and low level performance for each dimension.

Harrell and Wright (1990) tested the validity and reliability of the Wright (1986) BARS system in appraisals of 216 junior staff by 152 appraisers from senior up to partner level, together with further questionnaire data gathered from the appraisers. Their results suggested some minor amendment to the Wright (1986) model in terms of content validity,[207] but the construct validity of the system was confirmed by the strength and nature of the relationship between the appraisal ratings and various relevant measures, for example annual salary increases, promotion to a higher staffing level, whether it was desired to retain staff and involuntary departure from the firm. By comparison with the conventional performance appraisal scales in use in the firm under study, the appraisers considered that the BARS system provided a more complete indication of the factors determining auditor performance and a more accurate assessment of actual performance.

Appraisals on individual assignments are only one part, albeit a very important one, of the overall process which determines how the performance of an individual auditor is evaluated. Within the formal appraisal system are feedback interviews with senior personnel charged with human resource responsibilities, while there may also be input from training personnel. In the UK the ability to pass the professional examinations in a timely fashion is also likely to be relevant. More informally, a network of perceptions as to individuals as 'high-flyers' or otherwise is likely to develop from an early stage and this too is likely to influence appraisal and promotion.[208] Research to date has focused primarily on the assignment appraisals but one study, that of Kida (1984), did focus on review meetings between seniors and managers as part of the

---

[207] Specifically a reduction to three categories of performance dimension with *interpersonal skills* being subsumed within *professional characteristics* and working papers moving from the category *technical and analytical skills* to that of *communication skills.*

[208] Anderson-Gough *et al.* (1998, p.61) reported that 'trainees often perceived the appraisal forms to be more ritualistic than substantive: salary and promotion prospects were seen more often to be signalled through much less formal relationships and assessments within the firm.'

appraisal system, investigating the characteristics of these meetings which contributed to the satisfaction of the parties concerned with the meetings and to seniors' perceptions of the likelihood of improved subsequent performance. In line with findings reported in the wider human resource management literature,[209] it was found that the greater the involvement of the seniors in the meeting and their participation in goal setting the more likely it was that both parties would be satisfied with the outcome of the meeting. However, greater participation did not lead to increased perceptions of improved performance. Contrary to studies outside the accounting field, which suggested that there was little if any correlation between criticism by the reviewer and improved subsequent performance of the reviewee, Kida found that specific job related (as compared to personal) criticism was the factor which contributed most to reviewees' perceptions that their performance would improve.

Summary

- **There are differences between appraisers and appraisees within firms in respect to the importance placed on separate appraisal criteria, but there is little evidence that these differences are reflected in terms of perceptions of performance.**
- **At lower levels within the firm perceived technical skill is the appraisal criterion which has the greatest impact on performance evaluation. At higher levels within the firm technical skill assumes much less importance as a factor in performance evaluation.**
- **More systematic and structured appraisal systems, for example Behaviourally Anchored Rating Scales, allow a more complete indication of the factors determining the assessment of an auditor's performance and a more accurate assessment of that performance.**
- **Formal appraisal systems are only one aspect within a wider network of informal appraisal, assessments and relationships which feedback into an overall perception of an individual's performance and prospects.**

[209] See Nemeroff and Wexley (1979).

4.10 Determinants of Job Performance

Job Performance Models

Appraisal of job performance is likely to play an important role both in determining career paths and patterns within accounting firms, and as a feedback mechanism which highlights areas in which performance can be improved. However, perhaps more fundamental are questions as to those factors, individual and environmental, which influence and shape the manner in which duties and tasks are carried out. Analogous to the development of the research into actual and intended turnover, two strands of research can be detected in respect to determinants of job performance. The first focuses primarily on constructs which might be termed exogenous, for example innate personality dispositions, levels of education, gender etc. and seeks to ascertain whether there are associations between these constructs and the level of job performance. The second relates job performance more directly to aspects and issues which are at least in part controllable by the employer organization. Investigation of the means whereby employees can be motivated to exert additional effort may provide a basis for structures and reward mechanisms which will enhance effort, motivation and job performance. Again, analogous to the research on turnover and turnover intentions, many of the studies bridge across the two strands of research, for example expectancy studies of motivation may utilise exogenous variables, such as educational achievement, as moderating variables.

One issue confronting researchers in this field has been how to measure the quality of job performance. The majority of studies have focused on performance appraisal by those more advanced within the hierarchy, whether in terms of appraisal on individual assignments or an overall appraisal, as an appropriate yardstick. As an alternative or additional measure some studies have relied on self appraisal measures of effort and performance,[210] others on more objective measures such as salary levels and speed of advancement through the firm. One would expect all these measures to be closely correlated although there has been some conflicting evidence in this respect.[211]

---

210 Jiambalvo (1979) suggests that seniors' self appraisals are more reliable than appraisal by superiors because they are less likely to be influenced by 'halo' effects.

211 Choo (1986) observed a high product moment correlation, $r = 0.86$, between self and firm ratings, whereas in the Harrell and Stahl (1984) study the correlation was quite low, r

A number of studies have investigated whether there is a relationship between prior academic achievement, in particular the possession of a higher degree, and better job performance. Studies by Ferris (1981, 1982a) and Ross and Ferris (1981) found little evidence of association between the type of degree obtained, the grades obtained, or the rating of the educational establishment attended and the overall performance rating for either junior or senior auditors. However, a series of studies authored or co-authored by Siegel[212] did suggest a significant link between the nature and type of prior educational achievement and job performance. Over time auditors with a Masters degree in accounting achieved superior performance evaluations to those with just a Bachelors degree in accounting, whose evaluations were in turn superior to those who possessed a Bachelors degree other than in accounting. One factor specifically investigated by Siegel *et al.* (1992) was whether internship (work experience in a public accounting firm while still at university) was associated with subsequent better performance. The results showed that for auditors possessing only a Bachelors degree but who had internship experience the gap between their performance and that of auditors who possessed a Master's degree was greatly reduced. Siegel *et al.* attribute this result to the value of internships in socialising students into public practice.

Other characteristics, wholly or partly exogenous, investigated by Ferris (1981) included: willingness to exert effort, organizational commitment, desire to maintain organizational membership, task related ability, age, marital status, social background, and measures of physical attractiveness (height, weight and facial attractiveness). Although a number of statistically significant associations held across samples of junior and senior auditors there was no strong overall consistency in that the majority of factors which were positively associated with job performance for one group of auditors did not have any clear relationship to the performance of the other group and vice versa. For example, for audit juniors' age and marital status were associated with better job performance, but these factors had no clear links with performance at the

---

= 0.38. Surprisingly, Ferris and Larcker (1983) found little correlation between performance ratings and salary levels for the junior audit staff in their study, a result they attribute to salary levels being anchored on initial entry level pay.

212 Siegel (1987), Siegel and Rigsby (1988), Siegel and Spiceland (1988) and Siegel *et al.* (1992).

senior level.[213] Similarly, factors such as the desire to maintain organizational membership and type of social background which were associated with better job performance for seniors, were not so associated for juniors.[214] Of course in part this may reflect that both perceptions and the actuality of performance change as individuals rise up the hierarchy and that different factors do come into play at separate stages of career development.

Rebele *et al.* (1996) sought to relate job performance to the stages of an individual's career and reported that job performance in the first two career stages, those of exploration and establishment, was significantly lower than in the next two stages, maintenance and disengagement, with performance being at its highest in the disengagement stage.[215] In this study a self rating measure of performance was used and it is open to conjecture whether the same result would hold if a different measurement method was employed.

Rebele and Michaels (1990) examined the relationship between stress related variables and performance. They found that role ambiguity and perceived environmental uncertainty were significantly and negatively related to job performance, although role conflict had no significant effect. These relationships were not moderated by either the organizational level of the respondent or their perceived need for achievement. More recently Fisher (2001) reported both role ambiguity and role conflict to be negatively related to job performance whereas having a Type A personality was positively related to job performance. Choo (1986 and 1995) investigated the hypothesis that as stress levels increased performance initially improved and then as stress overload cut in performance levels fell. The results of both of the studies supported this hypothesis. In the laboratory experiment reported in Choo (1995) this pattern was observed both in relation to specific audit task-related mental stress and task-related judgement performance and in relation to overall job-related stress and job-related judgement performance.

---

[213] Fogarty (1996) found that married auditors outperformed single auditors at both the junior and senior level. He suggests that this may be attributable to a higher level of maturity and ability to concentrate consquent to the additional stability in their personal lives.

[214] Ross and Ferris (1981) also reported inconsistencies in the determinants of performance of audit juniors and seniors.

[215] See p.53 for a description of these career stages.

Hyatt and Prawitt (2001) investigated the interactions between audit firm structure, auditors' internal or external locus of control[216] and job performance. In accordance with their expectations the results of the study showed that auditors performed at a higher level when the firm structure and the auditor's locus of control were compatible. Specifically externally orientated auditors in highly structured firms performed at a higher level than externally orientated auditors in unstructured firms, whereas internally orientated auditors in unstructured firms performed at a higher level than internally orientated auditors in structured firms.

One early study which focused on a rather different determinant of job performance was that of Blocher (1979). This study investigated the relationship between audit assignment scheduling and performance. Based on audit managers' overall evaluations there was no evidence of change in the performance of audit seniors when they carried out consecutive assignments at the same audit client. When audit seniors carried out a series of assignments in different industries performance levels too remained unchanged but, perhaps surprisingly, when seniors undertook consecutive assignments within the same industry there was an initial decline in performance although performance subsequently improved with further assignments.

Given the perceived wisdom that continuity in terms of either client or industry should to some extent enhance auditor performance these results are of interest. However, as Blocher counseled it may be that managers implicitly discount these learning curve effects in their performance appraisal as they expect the audit to be conducted more efficiently.

A family of models of varying degrees of sophistication have been developed under the general heading of expectancy theory (Vroom, 1964). The essential thrust of these models is that the motivation of an individual to exert effort is a function of their perception that this effort will lead to enhanced performance across certain measurable dimensions *(expectancy)*, their belief that in turn this enhanced performance will lead to rewards *(instrumentality)*, and that these rewards, monetary or non-monetary, will possess value to them *(valence)*. Typically, *expectancy*, *instrumentality* and *valence* are measured by means of questionnaire responses and

---

216 Individuals with an internal locus of control believe that outcomes are determined by their own actions while individuals with an external locus of control believe that outcomes are determined by factors outside their control.

aggregated to establish a measure of effort.[217] Job performance is then modelled as a function of effort although this relationship may be moderated by other variables, for example measures of individual ability and of organizational commitment. Studies which may be grouped under this heading include those of Ferris (1977b), Ferris (1978), Jiambalvo (1979), Ferris *et al.* (1980), Ferris and Larcker (1983), Murray and Frazier (1986) and Moizer and Pratt (1988).

The results of these studies have been mixed. Ferris (1977b) suggested that the results of his study 'cast considerable doubt upon the ability of the expectancy model to explain productivity variations among staff accountants....; they also question the utility of the theory in a professional setting.'[218] Murray and Frazier (1986) too concluded that the:

> wide variance in the magnitude and significance of the results across subjects suggests that the expectancy model operationalized and tested here was a poor predictor of the effort and performance of some of the subjects we studied.[219]

In his (1977b) study Ferris modelled job performance as a function of ability, role perceptions as to how relevant types of work pattern were to the task in question, and motivation. He found that the model explained only a small part of the variance in the dependent variable, with only ability and role perception being significant in their effect. He noted that: 'The primary expectancy variable, motivation, was found to have an insignificant path coefficient and to make a trivial net contribution to the explained variation.'[220] Ferris (1978) incorporated uncertainty into the model (and changed the performance measure from one based upon peer evaluation to one based upon superior evaluation). He found that the expectancy that effort leads to goal accomplishment varied significantly with the perceived level of uncertainty. Auditors who perceived lower levels of uncertainty had higher levels of motivation than those perceiving higher levels of uncertainty and the association between motivation and job performance decreased as uncertainty increased.

Ferris *et al.* (1980) used an expectancy model to compare Australian and US audit juniors and seniors. Relatively few significant differences

---

[217] The appropriate method by which combination and aggregation should take place has been subject to investigation, see Jiambalvo (1979).
[218] p.613.
[219] p.403.
[220] p.612.

were found across the majority of expectancy, instrumentality, valence and motivation scores although US auditors placed greater value on opportunities for advancement than Australian auditors. In terms of the relationship to performance the results were more mixed. Four separate performance measures were utilised: current salary level, an overall evaluation based on a recent audit engagement, an evaluation relative to other auditors, and an assessment of partnership potential (the last three being provided by a recent supervisor). Effort was significantly related to overall and relative performance only for the US sample and to partnership potential only for the Australian sample.

Jiambalvo (1979) used an expectancy type model to investigate aspects of the role of the internal performance appraisal system in promoting enhanced effort and improved performance. Separate models were run for three different dependent variables. These were audit seniors' perception of their effort across nine appraisal related dimensions, audit seniors' perceptions of their performance across these dimensions on recent assignments, and their managers perceptions of the audit seniors' performance across these dimensions on these assignments. The expectancy related independent variables were: the expectancy that effort leads to effective performance on the nine evaluation dimensions; the expectancy that being effective on the evaluation dimensions leads to being judged as effective on that dimension; the expectancy that being judged on the evaluation dimensions contributes to a high overall evaluation of performance; the instrumentality of a high overall evaluation of performance for the attainment of a job outcome (in terms of pay, promotion, advancement etc.); the desirability of such a job outcome; and the intrinsic desirability of engaging in activities related to evaluation dimensions.

The results showed that all these variables were significant in relation to audit seniors' perceptions of their effort and performance. Similarly, all were significant in relation to managers' perceptions of audit senior performance with the exception of the variable identifying the intrinsic desirability of engaging in activities related to the evaluation dimension (which might broadly be described as a variable measuring how much the audit senior enjoyed his or her work).

In a rare example of a subsequent study utilising data from an earlier study but making methodological adjustments, Murray and Frazier (1986) used the underlying data from Jiambalvo (1979) but tested the model using a within-subject, rather than a between-subject, research design. It has been argued that a within-subject design is more consistent with the inherent focus of expectancy theory on individual choice.[221] The results did show rather stronger average explanatory power which the authors considered increased the credibility of the model but, as noted above, overall the model was only moderately successful in terms of explaining either effort or performance.

Ferris and Larcker (1983) extended the work of Ferris (1977b) and Jiambalvo (1979) and incorporated organizational commitment, task related ability, and measures of interpersonal attraction between the rater and the ratee into their performance model which used audit juniors as subjects. The dependent variable, job performance, was measured alternatively by current salary, most recent annual performance rating, and an assessment relative to other auditors from the most recently completed audit engagement. The results differed according to the form of the dependent variable. Salary levels were positively related to measures of task related ability (essentially prior educational achievement) and physical attractiveness whereas the other two measures of performance were positively associated with organizational commitment and motivation.

In their UK study Moizer and Pratt (1988) modelled a number of self perceived performance related measures[222] in terms of ability, effort and luck (also based on the self perceptions of the subjects of the study). Their results suggested that ability, effort and luck were significantly associated with the level of performance but that the overall predictive power of the model was not all that high. Furthermore, the model was not robust across the range of performance related measures applied.

Attribution Theory

A number of studies have sought to ascertain how appraisers develop causal explanations for perceived events, for example a time overrun on an assignment. Attribution theory, which is based on the assumption that

---

[221] See Kopelman (1983) and Schepanski *et al.* (1992) for further discussion of the relevant issues as applicable respectively to expectancy theory models and behavioural accounting research more generally.

[222] Specifically perception of an effectiveness in helping the firm to achieve its goals, of the individual's performance relative to that of other members of the firm, and of the likelihood of promotion.

individuals seek to interpret events rationally (Kelley, 1973), suggests that following an untoward event individuals seek informational cues as to why it has happened in order that they can attribute a cause to the event. This attribution may be internal, effectively when an individual is blamed or praised for the relevant event, or external, when environmental factors beyond the individual's control are seen as responsible.

In a series of papers, Kaplan and Reckers (1985, 1991 and 1993) sought to test the application of this theory in the context of the appraisal of the performance of audit seniors. The underlying methodology in all three studies was that subjects were provided with a scenario[223] in which an audit senior had both exceeded time budget and missed a client imposed deadline on an assignment. Subjects were provided with further additional information, for example as to the nature of the audit senior's previous work history and as to the audit firm's previous relationship with the client. Given the scenario and variations of the additional information, subjects were asked to assess separately internal causal attributions in terms of the effort, leadership ability, decision making ability and intrinsic motivation of the senior, and external attributions in terms of task difficulty, client co-operation, staff effort and ability, and luck. Subjects were also asked to assess whether appropriate subsequent action would focus on seeking to influence positively the senior's attitude and level of effort, or on factors relating to the client and audit scheduling.

Kaplan and Reckers (1985) found that both previous poor work history of the audit senior and the existence of a stable auditor-client relationship were significantly associated with higher internal attributions. In terms of response higher internal attribution was strongly correlated with action designed to influence the audit senior, whereas high external attributions were more weakly correlated with proposed action to change environmental factors. There were no significant differences between seniors and managers in terms of attribution suggesting to the authors that 'managers and seniors do not have significantly different perspectives concerning the cause(s) of a senior's sub-standard performance.'[224]

In Kaplan and Reckers (1991) the information as to the senior auditor's previous work history was varied so that instead of distinguishing between a good and bad previous history it distinguished between consistent and

---

[223] The study design varied in that in Kaplan and Reckers (1985) each subject was provided with two versions of the additional information, whereas in Kaplan and Reckers (1993) each subject only received one version.

[224] p.485.

inconsistent previous performance both around an overall favourable rating. Again the stability or otherwise of the relationship with the client was an important factor in determining whether attributions were internal or external, but the consistency of previous performance of the audit senior had little impact. In contrast to their earlier study there were differences in attributions according to the experience of the rater, the more experienced the rater the more likely it was that an internal rather than external attribution would be made.[225]

Subjects were asked to select a proposed course of action within a range of possibilities but as almost all subjects elected to counsel and to advise, no variation could be associated with differing attributions. However, attributions were linked to the likelihood that the audit senior would be sought after to work on a future audit (more likely if the sub-standard performance was attributed to task difficulty and less likely if it was attributed to lack of audit senior ability) and to the likelihood that the rater (subject) would request that the auditor worked on an audit for which he or she was responsible (more likely if the sub-standard performance was attributed to task difficulty). The authors suggest that this may be indicative of a preference for informal rather than formal mechanisms for communication and feedback within the organization.

Attribution theory has been criticised because of its treatment of the person being evaluated as a passive player in the process.[226] Kaplan and Reckers (1993) suggest that this is particularly inappropriate in the audit context in which individuals are aware that their work will be evaluated and will interact in that process. In their study they investigated whether explanation by the audit senior of the reasons for the time and budget overrun influenced attributions and also the manner in which causal attributions influenced specific appraisal decisions. Subjects[227] were provided with the basic scenario with or without the senior's justification for the time and budget overrun, together with information documenting improving or worsening job performance over the audit senior's previous nine assignments and identifying the client as in either a strong or weak financial condition.

---

[225] Kaplan and Reckers note that the 1991 study used a finer measure based on the number of years working for a public accounting firm rather than a senior/manager dichotomy as the basis for this variable.
[226] Kelley and Michela (1980).
[227] Whereas their previous two studies used seniors and managers as subjects, this study used only seniors.

The results suggested that the presence of an explanation had a significant effect in shifting causal attributions to external rather than internal factors. Surprisingly, this effect was not moderated by the other information, as similar cognizance was taken of an explanation from an audit senior with a deteriorating work record at a financially healthy client as of an explanation from a senior with an improving work record at a financially distressed client. Less surprisingly, attributions were significantly related to overall end of assignment performance, evaluations with high internal attributions being associated with a lower overall rating. As in their earlier study, high internal attributions were negatively associated with the rater's desire to work with the audit senior on a future assignment and high external attributions were positively associated with such an intention.

Johnson *et al.* (1996) manipulated both the nature of the explanation and the gender of the audit senior in their investigation of performance evaluation in the circumstances of a significant time budget overrun. Their results showed that their subjects rated the performance of female audit seniors below that of male audit seniors and also that performance ratings were lower when the explanation of the overrun was couched in terms of domestic illness than when it related to client failure to generate work schedules.

Summary

- **There is some evidence that auditors with educational qualifications at the Masters level and above perform better than those with undergraduate degrees alone, but the evidence is mixed. There is also evidence that at lower staffing levels performance ratings are higher when staff have experience of working in a public accounting firm while at university.**
- **As stress levels increase the job performance of individual auditors initially improves but beyond a certain level of stress measures of job performance begin to decline again.**
- **There has been extensive effort to seek to model the motivation and job performance of individual auditors by reference to their expectations that greater effort on their behalf will lead to greater rewards with value to them. To date these models, derived from the**

wider human resource management literature, have been relatively unsuccessful in their application to auditors.

5 Conclusions

The studies whose findings are reported in the ten sections of Chapter 4 represent a significant body of research covering many varied aspects of human resource issues within accounting and audit firms. In this brief concluding chapter our intention is to bring together and highlight certain of these research results; to discuss the contribution of the research that has been carried out to date; and to make some suggestions as to the direction that might be taken by future researchers in this field. Rather than separately summarise again the research findings on a section by section basis we seek here to develop themes relevant to the process of human resource management in large accounting and audit firms, and to illuminate and enhance our discussion by reference to ideas and perspectives derived from the interviews with personnel with human resource management responsibilities in these firms in the UK.

Career Development

Personal Attitudes and Characteristics

Many of the studies have charted associations between a range of individual personal attitudes and characteristics and measures of job satisfaction, propensity to suffer stress, the likelihood of success in terms of promotion and advancement. Attitudes and characteristics associated with success include: above average needs for achievement and power, influence orientation - in the sense of a belief in one's ability to change things and make things happen, a high level of ascendancy and sociability, and physical attractiveness.

Certain of these attitudes and characteristics are those which in the organizational behaviour and psychology literature are traditionally deemed masculine. A number of studies have highlighted the low proportion of women in the higher reaches of accounting and audit firms, as compared with the almost equal numbers of men and women who join the firms as recruits, and these studies suggest that the perceptions and realities of accounting and audit firms as male dominated organizations have contributed to this disparity. The interviews carried out with senior personnel holding human resource management responsibilities in accounting and audit firms confirmed the importance of gender related issues to the UK firms, but there were different views as to whether the relatively low numbers of women advancing to partnership level, or its equivalent, indicated a failure in human resource management terms or whether this was a result of individual and societal characteristics largely beyond the control of the firms.

Education and Examinations

There has been extensive research in North America focusing on linkages between prior educational achievement and career development within accounting and audit firms. The results of these studies have not been wholly conclusive but they do suggest that education at more highly rated educational institutions and the possession of a higher degree are both associated with more rapid career development in terms of pay and promotion.

There are significant differences between the UK and the USA in terms of the structure of higher education and the professional examination process and caution must be exercised in interpreting and applying the results of the US research in the UK context. There has for many years been a clear perception within the UK firms of a connection between good 'A' level scores and the likelihood of passing professional examinations, and this has been a significant factor in their recruitment policies. In contrast, prior academic study of accounting has been perceived as relatively unimportant. There is scope here for further investigation of the linkages between educational attributes and professional examination success against the background of the recent changes in the ICAEW examination structure.

In the UK passing the professional examinations in a timely fashion is still seen as a necessary hurdle to be overcome if success is to be achieved within audit, but as individuals rise through the hierarchy of their firm skills in terms of marketing, management and leadership become increasingly more valued, and technical competence *per se* relatively less important.

Acculturation and Socialisation

The process of acculturation and socialisation which begins when new recruits join the firm is heavily influenced by learning from, and observation of, peers and immediate superiors. From an early stage individuals come to appreciate the need to deploy their particular skills and personality traits within an organizational ethos which places an emphasis on conformity to type. In the development of client related skills and in the interaction with other members of the organization, emulation of others in terms of how they think, act and even look is important.

The pyramidic staff structure, and the expectation of many recruits that they will leave within a relatively short time frame after qualification, suggests that organizational commitment is likely to be relatively low until individuals perceive the possibility of a longer term career within the firm. Over time the acculturation process does appear to lead to enhanced organizational commitment, but the extent to which professional commitment develops and the extent to which professional commitment can in fact be distinguished from organizational commitment is less clear. It can be argued that in accounting and auditing the concept of being a professional has little meaning outside an organizational context. Accountants and auditors in the large firms derive much of their understanding of the term professional from the values and culture pervasive in those firms. Other than in the setting of examinations, the professional bodies intrude little, if at all, in the process of professionalisation. This may have advantages from a human resource management perspective in that the potential for tension between the organizational imperatives of client service and growth and more traditional professional values, with their emphasis on ethics and public service, is likely to be reduced. It does however raise wider issues as to the nature of professionalism in accounting and auditing and of the relationship between the large firms and the professional bodies.

One aspect of the process of career development which has received relatively little research attention is that of the role of formal training within the firm. At lower levels in the firm this training is likely to focus on specific techniques and audit approaches and may interrelate with preparation for professional examinations. At higher levels training courses for new managers and partners will focus on issues such as appraisal, team management, leadership, client management and the internal management structure and organization of the firm. Certain of the studies reviewed in this monograph have touched on aspects of the role of formal training, for example one study suggested that internal documentation, manuals etc. were less important as information sources than questioning of peers and superiors whereas in another the lack of formal training provided in respect to appraisal techniques was highlighted, but there have been few studies which have focused directly on the role and function of training *per se*.

Traditionally formal career development and guidance mechanisms within the firms took second place to more immediate needs in terms of scheduling, staff availability etc. In such circumstances informal mentoring procedures assumed great importance in aiding and guiding an individual's career path within the firm. In the much larger firms of today there are more formal mechanisms for counselling and support, more opportunity for transfer and mobility and a greater transparency in promotion procedures. How effective these are in achieving their objectives and the extent to which they have supplanted more informal procedures with their emphasis on networking and patronage are interesting questions.

Staffing Patterns

Perhaps the single most distinctive feature of human resource management in accounting and audit firms is the pyramidic staffing structure whereby each year large numbers of very able graduates are recruited[228] of whom only a small proportion will in time achieve partnership status within the firm. The path to partnership has traditionally been clearly defined in terms of a series of promotions at relatively predetermined stages. At almost every stage failure to achieve the relevant promotion in a timely fashion signals that the individual's chances of attaining partnership are remote.

---

[228] In 1999 more than three quarters of the UK graduates registering for training contracts with the ICAEW possessed a first or upper second class honours degree (ICAEW, 2000, p.3).

Although there has for many years been questioning as to the economic efficacy of this model[229] it has proved to be a resilient one and still forms the basic staffing pattern in the large firms today. However, the interviewees did suggest that it is becoming less rigid in its application and that a greater flexibility of career pattern is opening up, including the possibility of longer term careers within the firms for those who do not achieve partnership or equivalent status.

One factor contributing to this change has been the relative diminution of the importance of audit and audit related services within the overall range of services provided by the firms. The pyramidic staffing structure is essentially a construct of audit. Employment patterns in taxation and consulting have always been different, although in the past these differences have been partially obscured by the significant transfers of personnel from audit to taxation and, to a lesser extent, to consulting. As other functional areas within the firm have assumed an increasing importance and profile a staffing pattern predicated on the particular needs of audit has become open to challenge.

However, there have also been doubts raised as to the suitability of the model in respect to audit. The changing nature of financial controls and the ever increasing sophistication of financial information systems has prompted the firms to ask searching questions as to future development of audit and audit related services. Some firms have identified an increasing dichotomy between the more routine tasks associated with audit and those which require specific high level skills. This in turn raises questions as to the suitability of a pattern of recruitment geared to the employment and training of able (and relatively expensive) generalists.

Other factors which have acted to disturb the rigidity of the structure have been a greater willingness of the firms to provide opportunities for career breaks and a willingness to countenance part-time work for professional staff, changes which have in part been a response to the much higher proportion of women working for the firms. The changing nature of management and control within the firms may also be relevant, titles and status are no longer as rigidly defined and the achievement of partnership is not necessarily the sole yardstick by which success is measured internally.

---

[229] In particular there have been perennial concerns as to the cost of employing and training such large numbers of staff whose tenure in the firm is relatively short, and as to the problems of planning, scheduling and ensuring continuity of client service against a background of such high staff turnover.

It would be wrong to exaggerate the extent and nature of this change, as yet it has been tentative, but there may be the beginnings of a significant paradigm shift toward what many would see from a human resource management viewpoint as a more conventional and cost effective staffing structure.

The Multi-Disciplinary Global Firm

In recent years the large accounting and audit firms have come to see themselves, and to market themselves, as global professional services conglomerates. Even within the traditional functional disciplines of audit, taxation and consultancy there is today a vast array of different service provision.[230] However, the pressures toward the break-up of these firms are strong, both internally from the desire of the existing partners to realise the market value which has been built up as their activities have developed far beyond the fields of accounting and audit, and externally from the desire of regulators, in particular the SEC in the USA, to promote and enforce a clearer separation of audit from other activities. A number of the large firms have sought, or are actively considering, partial demerger by selling-off their consultancy operations. The question does arise of whether these firms will seek to re-enter the markets that they are presently vacating. The Hydra-like success of Arthur Andersen (now Andersen) in developing a significant consulting presence within a fairly short space of time following the split from Andersen Consulting (now Accenture) may encourage other firms to consider similar auto-regeneration and, notwithstanding the present turbulence within the large firms, it does seem likely that they will still be characterised by a significant element of multi-disciplinarity in future years. In this context one area of potential research interest lies in the manner in which firms seek to accommodate and integrate the varying cultures across the functions and lines of business within which they operate. Among these actual or potential cultural differences are those in relation to patterns of professionalism, and perceptions of image, profile and potential for growth.

---

[230] For example, PricewaterhouseCoopers built up an 'HR solutions group' comprising some 6,000 people worldwide. Specialists within the group include 'lawyers', taxation experts, pay and reward specialists, human resource consultants and actuaries.' (PricewaterhouseCoopers, 1998).

Here a number of questions arise as to the role of the human resource management function in accommodating and perhaps encouraging particular ways of doing business within the various functional areas while at the same time presenting to the outside world an impression of unity in terms of the external image. In the past the forces acting to preserve the unity of purpose within the firms, for example the benefits of trading under a particular 'brand', the substantial overlap between audit and non-audit services in terms of their client base, and the constraints of the partnership structure have been powerful enough to contain the strong in-built fissiparous tendencies. As the firms have grown and their organizational structures have changed arguably these forces have weakened relative to those which prompt demerger and divestment. The role of the human resource management function both as an actor and to an extent an arbitrator in this contest is an important one and its role both in terms of the identification of appropriate management models and personnel policies within the functional areas and more generally as an agent for, or an impediment to, change is one which merits further study.

Analogous to the problems posed by the multi-disciplinary nature of large accounting and audit firms are those which arise in consequence of globalisation. Here again there are forces, for example the need to achieve an equivalent level of service in all countries, the need to integrate the work force on an international basis, which call for an essential uniformity in the practice of human resource management across the firms worldwide. However, there are clear differences in the commercial and cultural environments within which the various national firms work. These differences include those relating to education and professional qualification, for example the route to qualification in Continental Europe is typically much slower and more specialised than that in the UK (and the USA), a gamut of variations of commercial and professional practice and of legal form and structure,[231] as well as wider economic and societal factors.

Some of the firms have sought to develop uniform grading structures for staff on a worldwide basis but typically they have confronted difficulty in obtaining agreement at national level and progress in this direction has been slow. The advantages of identical structures are seen in terms of engendering unity of purpose on an international basis as well as their relevance to more practical issues of transfer and secondment of staff

[231] Including, as one interviewee pointed out, significant differences in employment law.

between countries. The need to service clients on an international basis is likely to strengthen the pressures for greater uniformity but there are significant obstacles to the introduction of common human resource management practices worldwide.

Management Structure and Practice

The management structure of the large firms has shifted away from the traditional partnership model to bear a much closer resemblance to the styles and structures of organizational control employed by their corporate clients. The increasing importance of 'management' as a function in its own right raises questions as to possible tensions between the providers of professional services and those who seek to manage and organize that provision. These issues are not of course unique to accounting and audit firms but arise across an array of service providers, perhaps most notably in the health service and education. In these public service organizations the rise of the professional manager has given rise to concerns as to the locus of power and control within the organization, and as to the validity of judgements made by those other than with specific expertise, for example in terms of clinical judgements.

Here areas for further study include the nature and practice of 'managerialism' within the firms on both a national and international basis and the extent to which managerial power has been retained by professionals in accounting and audit, widely defined, and the extent to which it has been usurped by 'managers' who are not themselves specialists in the services provided by accounting and audit firms. Here we would observe that there has been some variation across the firms in the formulation and implementation of these organizational changes. For example, there are significant differences between the firms in terms of the responsibilities, staffing and visibility of the human resource management function itself. We would also observe that, as compared with public sector organizations, control and power in accounting and audit firms has been retained by partners, or those with equivalent status, emanating from a client service background. In accounting and audit firms the direct link between revenue, profitability and client management means that internal credibility and power still resides with those individuals who are or to an extent have been 'client facing'. This contrasts with, for example, the situation in health and education where the link between the service providers and income is much more diffuse and in consequence professional 'management' is far more powerful.

Although in terms of persona the locus of control has not shifted to the extent that it has in some other service providing organizations, 'management' in terms of the setting of targets, rewarding success in reaching those targets and penalising failure has been enthusiastically embraced by the large firms. One factor which has contributed to a culture with an intensive focus on the attainment of short term performance targets has been the perception within the firms that growth of revenue and partnership income is the overriding imperative. Failure to exceed or at least match the growth of competitor firms is perceived as likely to result in loss of status, loss of clients and make the entity vulnerable to takeover. Here again there are a number of questions as to how this key emphasis on growth and the achievement of targets in terms of income and profitability interacts with other professed longer term management objectives, for example, developing and portraying both internally and externally particular sets of values in terms of quality, culture and ethics.

The Value of Research

A final issue that we address is that of the impact of the academic research that has taken place on professional practice. In his review of the voluminous research literature on audit judgements Trotman (1998) suggests that this body of research has had a significant impact on practice. We would suggest that to make such a claim in the context of research into human resource management would be problematic and indeed hard to justify in so far as it relates to the UK. The direct impact of the research has been minimal, although the human resource personnel that we interviewed were keenly interested in many of the issues covered by the studies reviewed none of them professed an awareness of this body of research. Nor did they consider that others in their firm would have such an awareness. Whether there have been indirect influences, either in terms of research findings feeding through into the more mainstream human resource management and general business journals, or via ideas and influences from the North American practices is more difficult to gauge although we would suggest that any such influences have been at best muted and diffuse.

Implicitly at least, the issues identified in Chapter 3 in terms of the accessibility, focus and timeliness of academic research in accounting and auditing in general and the more specific concerns as to the methodology and North American orientation of the human resource management research have contributed to a situation where this research has been seen as of marginal relevance. In a paper delivered more than twenty years ago, Graham Stacy then Price Waterhouse's national technical partner suggested that the research needs of a professional firm 'can be satisfied almost entirely from its own resources' and that for a variety of reasons: familiarity with specific firm procedures, applicability to real world auditing and competitive confidentiality most firms do indeed prefer to carry out their own research.[232] We would consider that in the human resource management context this is still the perception held by the firms today.

This orientation perhaps adds weight to the suggestion that we make in Chapter 3 that there is scope for a shift in the ambitions and methodology of the research undertaken. In terms of research direction we would advocate a greater emphasis on the study of human resource management issues in accounting and audit firms from a wider sociological and organizational perspective. *Inter alia* this might entail study and analysis of the manner in which the unusual recruitment patterns and staffing structures of the large accounting and audit firms has contributed to and interacted with their sustained growth into the phenomenon which the multi-national and multi-functional professional services firms are today. It might include examination of the role of these firms as educators and trainers and their contribution to the wider commercial environment in terms of providing so many graduates with their first experience of the nature and realities of commerce and industry from a financial perspective. It might entail investigation of the meaning and nature of professionalism within these firms and explore the implications thereof.

Concomitant with a wider scope for research will be a need for more innovative methodological approaches with a greater willingness to employ techniques other than those rooted in the testing of significant associations on a statistical basis which underpin the great majority of academic studies to date. Devising and employing methodologies appropriate to a wider set of research questions will be a challenging task, but if successfully achieved we would envisage that it would enable this

---

[232] Quoted in Gwilliam (1987, p.27).

field of research to be of greater value both to the firms and to society more generally.

Appendix

Examples of studies published since 1970 of human resource management issues focusing specifically on auditing.

Author(s)	Journal	Auditor type	Research location	Type of audit firm	No. of auditor subjects
Addams (1981)	JA	Juniors	USA	1 Big 8 firms	164
Albrecht, Brown and Field (1981)	JA	All levels	USA	25 offices of different sized firms	Not stated
Alford, Strawser and Strawser (1990)	AH	Partners	USA	7 Big 8 firms	Not stated
Almer, Hopper and Kaplan (1998)	AH	Seniors, managers and partners	USA	Big 6 firms	45
Anderson, Johnson and Reckers (1994)	AOS	Not stated	USA	4 Big 6 and 1 national firm	120
Anderson-Gough, Grey and Robson (1998)	Book	Juniors	UK	2 offices of 2 Big 6 firms	77
Anderson-Gough, Grey and Robson (2001)	AOS	Juniors	UK	2 offices of 2 Big 6 firms	77
Bamber, Snowball and Tubbs (1989)	AR	Seniors	USA	Offices of 4 Big 8 firms	121
Belkaoui and Picur (1987)	JBFA	Seniors and managers	USA	2 Big 8 firms	231

Author(s)	Journal	Auditor type	Research location	Type of audit firm	No. of auditor subjects
Benke and Rhode (1980)	AOS	Seniors to partners	USA	Large CPA firms	126
Benke and Rhode (1984)	AA	Qualified CPAs	USA	Big 8 firms	126
Bhamornsiri and Guinn (1991)	IAE	Partners	USA	Big 6 firms	494
Blocher (1979)	AR	Seniors	USA	2 offices of 2 large firms	58
Charnes, Cooper, Detrick, Moody and Shin (1990)	AA	None	N/a	N/a	N/a
Choo (1986)	A:AJPT	Juniors to partners	Not stated	Large and small firms	172
		Juniors to partners	USA	Large and small firms	167
Choo (1995)	JAAF	All levels	Not stated	Not stated	252
		Seniors and managers	USA	International and regional firms	48
Dalton, Hill and Ramsey (1997)	A:AJPT	Managers and partners	USA	All Big 6 firms	205
Dillard (1976)	RBER	All levels	USA	Offices of 5 national and international firms	144
Dillard (1979)	AOS	All levels	USA	10 offices of 5 national firms	423
Dirsmith and Covaleski (1985)	AOS	All levels	USA	All Big 8 firms	110
Dirsmith, Heian and Covaleski (1997)	AOS	All levels	USA	All Big 6 firms	180

Author(s)	Journal	Auditor type	Research location	Type of audit firm	No. of auditor subjects
Earnest and Lampe (1982)	WCPA	Juniors and managers	USA	23 offices of large international firms	996
Earnest and Lampe (1987)	AA	Juniors to managers	USA	23 offices of large international firms	996
Emby and Etherington (1996)	A:AJPT	All levels	Canada	All big 6 firms in one city.	228
Ferris (1977a)	AOS	Juniors	USA	2 large firms	51
Ferris (1977b)	AR	Juniors	USA	2 Big 8 firms	51
Ferris (1978)	DS	Juniors	USA	2 large firms	51
Ferris (1981)	AOS	Juniors and seniors	USA	A large firm	123 juniors, and 46 seniors
Ferris (1982)	AOS	New hires, juniors and seniors	USA	A Big 8 firm	81 new hires, 123 juniors, and 46 seniors
Ferris, Dillard and Nethercott (1980)	AOS	Juniors and seniors	Australia	1 firm in each country and USA	45 in each country
Ferris and Larcker (1983)	AOS	Juniors	USA	An office of a Big 8 firm	90
Fisher (2001)	BRIA	All levels	New Zealand	2 Big 6 firms	119
Fogarty (1994)	MAJ	Juniors, semi-seniors and seniors	USA	Big 8 firms	460
Fogarty (1995)	BAR	Juniors	USA	Big 8 firms	460

Author(s)	Journal	Auditor type	Research location	Type of audit firm	No. of auditor subjects
Fogarty (1996)	MAJ	Juniors, semi-seniors and seniors	USA	Big 8 firms	460
Gaertner and Ruhe (1981)	JA	All levels	USA	2 offices of 3 national firms, and 1 office of 4 local or regional firms	193
Harrell (1990)	AA	6 months to 4 years after joining firm	USA	1 large firm	175
Harrell and Eickhoff (1988)	A:AJPT	Up to 30 months experience	USA	A large firm	175
Harrell and Wright (1990)	A:AJPT	Seniors to partners	USA	Offices of a national firm	152
Haskins, Baglioni and Cooper (1987)	CAR	Seniors	USA	1 Big 8 firm	168
Hermanson, Carcello, Hermanson, Milano, Polansky and Williams (1995)	JA	Juniors and partners	USA	5 Big 6 firms	371 juniors, 203 partners
Hood and Koberg (1991)	AH	All levels	USA	8 large firms	62
Hull and Umansky (1997)	AOS	Managers and partners	USA	9 national firms	959
Hyatt and Prawitt (2001)	AR	Juniors and Seniors	USA	4 Big 6 firms	375
Jeffrey, Weatherholt and Lo (1996)	IJA	All levels	Taiwan	Not stated	75

Author(s)	Journal	Auditor type	Research location	Type of audit firm	No. of auditor subjects
Jiambalvo (1979)	JAR	Seniors	USA	4 offices of a Big 8 firm	33
Jiambalvo (1982)	JAR	Seniors and partners	USA	3 offices of a large international firm	33 seniors, 17 partners
Jiambalvo and Pratt (1982)	AR	Juniors	USA	4 Big 8 firms	36
Jiambalvo, Watson and Baumler (1983)	AOS	Seniors to partners	USA	A major office of a large international firm	62
Johnson, Lowe and Reckers (1996)	AA	Seniors	USA	1 Big 6 firm	105
Kaplan, Keinath and Walo (2001)	BRIA	All levels	USA	Big 6, intermediate and local firms	242
Kaplan and Reckers (1985)	AR	Seniors and managers	USA	Offices of each of the Big 8 firms	60
Kaplan and Reckers (1991)	AA	Experienced auditors	USA	The Big 8 firms	107
Kaplan and Reckers (1993)	BRIA	Seniors	USA	A Big 6 firm	88
Kelley and Margheim (1990)	A:AJPT	Juniors and seniors	USA	2 offices of a Big 8 firm and 1 office of another Big 8 firm	85 pairs of juniors and seniors
Kida (1984)	AOS	Seniors and managers	USA	7 offices of 5 international firms	72

Author(s)	Journal	Auditor type	Research location	Type of audit firm	No. of auditor subjects
Lowe, Reckers and Sanders (2001)	IJAu	Seniors	USA	An international firm	95
Marxen (1996)	AH	Not stated	USA	Big 6 firms	121
Maupin (1990)	APIA	All levels	USA	Not stated	461
Maupin and Lehman (1994)	AOS	All levels	USA	Big 8 firms	461
Meuwissen (1998)	AE:AIJ	Qualified auditors	Nether-lands	Qualified auditors	642
Moizer and Pratt (1988)	ABR	Seniors and managers	UK	Large, medium and small firms	220
Morrison (1993a)	AMJ	Up to 6 months experience	USA	5 large firms	149 to 205
Morrison (1993b)	JAP	Up to 6 months experience	USA	5 large firms	135
Murray and Frazier (1986)	JAR	Seniors	USA	4 offices of a Big 8 firm	33
Norris and Niebuhr (1984)	AOS	All levels	USA	1 Big 8 firm	62
Otley and Pierce (1995)	AOS	Seniors	Ireland	3 Big 6 firms	275
Pasewark, Strawser and Wilkerson (1994)	AA	Juniors and managers	USA	2 Big 6 firms	49
Pratt and Beaulieu (1992)	AOS	Below partner level	USA	5 Big 8 firms, 3 regional firms and 2 local firms	338

Author(s)	Journal	Auditor type	Research location	Type of audit firm	No. of auditor subjects
Pratt and Jiambalvo (1981)	AOS	Audit team members (juniors to managers)	USA	4 offices of 4 national firms	36 audit teams
Pratt and Jiambalvo (1982)	AOS	Juniors and seniors	USA	4 Big 8 firms	48 juniors, 28 seniors
Purvis and Panich (1986)	CPAJ	Juniors	USA	Several firms	410
Rasch and Harrell (1990)	A:AJPT	All levels	USA	1 Big 8 firms	66
Rebele and Michaels (1990)	BRIA	All levels	USA	Offices of 4 large international firms	155
Rebele, Michaels and Wachter (1996)	AA	All levels	USA	4 international firms	157
Regel and Murray (1989)	AA	Juniors	USA	An office of a Big 8 firm	49
Robson, Wholey and Barefield (1996)	AMJ	Up to 5 years experience	USA	3 Big 8 firms	565
Ross and Ferris (1981)	ASQ	Juniors and seniors	USA	2 firms	26 to 114
Scandura and Viator (1994)	AOS	Managers and juniors	USA	Large accounting firms (including all Big 8 firms)	1024

Author(s)	Journal	Auditor type	Research location	Type of audit firm	No. of auditor subjects
Schloemer and Schloemer (1997)	AH	All levels	USA	1 office of a Big 8 firm, 1 office of one of the 12 largest firms and 2 small firms	125
Schroeder, Reinstein and Schwartz (1992)	AA	All levels	USA	10 offices of Big 8 firms	136
Senatra (1980)	AR	Seniors	USA	8 offices of a Big 8 firm	88
Senatra (1988)	WCPA	Seniors	USA	10 offices of a Big 8 firm	54 men, 37 women
Shaub, Finn and Munter (1993)	BRIA	Not stated	USA	4 offices of a national firm	207
Siegel (1987)	IAE	All levels	USA	5 international firms	455
Siegel, Blank and Rigsby (1991)	AAAJ	All levels	USA	12 offices of 4 Big 8 firms	751
Siegel and Rigsby (1988)	IAE	Juniors to managers	USA	3 international firms	Up to 1727
Siegel, Rigsby Agrawal and Leavins (1995)	AAAJ	All levels	USA	2 Big 6 firms	80
Siegel, Rigsby and Leavins (1992)	AA	Juniors to managers	USA	23 regional offices of 5 international firms	Up to 2037
Snead and Harrell (1991)	BRIA	Seniors	USA	A large firm	38

Author(s)	Journal	Auditor type	Research location	Type of audit firm	No. of auditor subjects
Spiceland, Siegel and George (1992)	AA	Up to 8 years experience	USA	27 regional offices of 5 international firms	621
Street, Schroeder and Schwartz (1993)	APIA	All levels	USA	4 large, 4 medium and 5 small firms	177
Wright (1982)	JAR	Seniors	USA	7 offices of Big 8 firms and 3 offices of large regional/ national firms	78
Wright (1985)	AA	Seniors	USA	7 offices of Big 8 firms and 3 offices of large regional/ national firms	78
Wright (1986)	A:AJPT	Juniors to supervisors	USA	3 offices of 3 national firms	35
Wright (1988)	AR	Semi-seniors to managers	USA	Offices of 5 Big 8 firms	110

Key:	AA	Advances in Accounting
	AAAJ	Accounting, Auditing and Accountability Journal
	A:AJPT	Auditing: A Journal of Practice & Theory
	ABR	Accounting and Business Research
	AE	Accounting Enquiries
	AE:AIJ	Accounting Education: An International Journal
	AH	Accounting Horizons
	AMJ	Academy of Management Journal
	AOS	Accounting, Organizations and Society
	APIA	Advances in Public Interest Accounting
	APJA	Asia-Pacific Journal of Accounting
	AR	The Accounting Review
	ASQ	Administrative Science Quarterly
	BAR	British Accounting Review
	BRIA	Behavioral Research in Accounting
	CAR	Contemporary Accounting Research
	CPAJ	CPA Journal
	DS	Decision Sciences
	IAE	Issues in Accounting Education
	IJA	International Journal of Accounting
	IJAu	International Journal of Auditing
	JA	Journal of Accountancy
	JAAF	Journal of Accounting, Auditing and Finance
	JAP	Journal of Applied Psychology
	JAR	Journal of Accounting Research
	JBFA	Journal of Business Finance and Accounting
	MAJ	Managerial Auditing Journal
	PR	Personnel Review
	RBER	Review of Business & Economic Research
	WCPA	The Woman CPA

Bibliography

Key:

$ Research published since 1970 relating to accountants in accounting and audit firms where the sample does include auditors, but separate results are not reported for the auditors sampled.

$$ Research published since 1970 relating to accountants working in accounting and audit firms for which auditors could be included in the sample.

$$$ Research published since 1970 relating to accountants working in a variety of work environments for which the sample includes accountants working in accounting and audit firms and could include auditors.

Abbott, A. 1988. *The System of Professions*. Chicago University Press.

Addams, H.L. 1981. Should the Big 8 teach communication skills? *Management Accounting* (USA), May, 37-40.

$$$ Adler, S. and N. Aranya. 1984. A comparison of the work needs, attitudes and preferences of professional accountants at different career stages. *Journal of Vocational Behavior*, August, pp. 45-57.

$$$ Adler, S., N. Aranya and J. Amernic. 1981. Community size, socialization and the work needs of professionals. *Academy of Management Journal*, September, pp. 504-511.

$$ Ahadiat, N. and J.J. Mackie. 1993. Ethics education in accounting: An investigation of the importance of ethics as a factor in the recruiting decisions of public accounting firms. *Journal of Accounting Education*, Fall, pp. 243-257.

$$ Ahadiat, N. and K.J. Smith. 1994. A factor analytic investigation of employee selection factors of significance to recruiters of entry level accountants. *Issues in Accounting Education*, Spring, pp. 59-79.

$ AICPA. 1990. *MAP Committee Survey on Professional Staff*. AICPA.

AICPA. 1997. *Report of the Special Committee on Assurance Services*. AICPA.

Albrecht, W.S., S.W. Brown and D.R. Field. 1981. Toward increased job satisfaction of practicing CPAs. *Journal of Accountancy*, August, pp. 61-66.

Alford, R.M., J.R. Strawser and R.H. Strawser. 1990. Does graduate education improve success in public accounting? *Accounting Horizons*, March, pp. 69-76.

Almer, E.D., J.R. Hopper and S.E. Kaplan. 1998. The effect of diversity-related attributes on hiring, advancement and voluntary turnover judgements. *Accounting Horizons*, March, pp. 1-17.

$$ Amernic, J.H., N. Aranya and J. Pollock. 1979. Is there a generally accepted standard accountant? How typical is the typical CA? *CA Magazine*, October, pp. 34-42.

$$$ Amernic, J.H., R. Kunungo and N. Aranya. 1983. Professional and work values of accountants: A cross-cultural study. *International Journal of Accounting*, Spring, pp. 177-192.

Anderson, J.C., E.N. Johnson and P.M.J. Reckers. 1994. Perceived effects of gender, family structure, and physical appearance on career progression in public accounting: A research note. *Accounting, Organizations and Society*, No. 6, pp. 483-491.

$$ Anderson Jr., T.N. and T.E. Kida. 1985. The effect of environmental uncertainty on the association of expectancy attitudes, effort, and performance. *The Journal of Social Psychology*, October, pp. 631-636.

$ Anderson-Gough, F., C. Grey and K. Robson. 1998. *Making Up Accountants: The Organizational and Professional Socialization of Trainee Chartered Accountants*. Ashgate.

$ Anderson-Gough, F., C. Grey and K. Robson. 2001. Tests of time reckoning and the making of accountants in two multi-national accounting firms. *Accounting, Organizations and Society*, March, pp. 99-122.

$$$ Aranya, N. and K.R. Ferris. 1983. Organizational-professional conflict among US and Israeli professional accountants. *The Journal of Social Psychology*, April, pp. 153-161.

$$ and $$$ Aranya, N. and K.R. Ferris. 1984. A reexamination of accountants' organizational-professional conflict. *The Accounting Review*, January, pp. 1-15.

$$$ Aranya, N., T. Kushnir and A. Valency. 1986. Organizational commitment in a male dominated profession. *Human Relations*, May, pp. 433-448.

$$ Aranya, N., R. Lachman and J. Amernic. 1982. Accountants' job satisfaction: A path analysis. *Accounting, Organizations and Society*, No. 3, pp. 201-215.

$$ Aranya, N., J. Pollock and J. Amernic. 1981. An examination of professional commitment in public accounting. *Accounting, Organizations and Society*, No. 4, pp. 271-280.

$$ Aranya, N., and J.T. Wheeler. 1986. Accountants' personality types and their commitment to organization and profession. *Contemporary Accounting Research*, No. 1, pp. 184-199.

$$$ Arnold, H.J. and D.C. Feldman. 1982. A multivariate analysis of the determinants of job turnover. *Journal of Applied Psychology*, June, pp. 350-360.

$$$ Arnold, H.J., D.C. Feldman and M. Purbhoo. 1985. The role of social-desirability response bias in turnover research. *Academy of Management Journal*, December, pp. 955-966.

$$ Aryee, S., T. Wyatt and M.K. Min. 1991. Antecedents of organizational commitment and turnover intentions among professional accountants in different employment settings. *The Journal of Social Psychology*, August, pp. 545-556.

Asare, S.K. and L.S. McDaniel. 1996. The effects of familiarity with the preparer and task complexity in the effectiveness of the audit review process. *The Accounting Review*, April, pp. 139-159.

Baker, C.R. 1977. Management strategy in a large accounting firm. *The Accounting Review*, July, pp. 576-585.

Bamber, E.M., D. Snowball and R.M. Tubbs. 1989. Audit structure and its relation to role conflict and role ambiguity: An empirical investigation. *The Accounting Review*, April, pp. 285-299.

$$$ Barcelona, C.T., C.C. Lelievre and T.H. Lelievre. 1975. The profession's underutilized resource: The woman CPA. *Journal of Accountancy*, November, pp. 58-64.

$ Barker, P.C. and K. Monks. 1998. Irish women accountants and career progression: A research note. *Accounting, Organizations and Society*, No. 8, pp. 813-823.

$$ Barker, P., K. Monks and F. Buckley. 1999. The role of mentoring in the career progression of chartered accountants. *The British Accounting Review*, September, pp. 297-312.

Barkman, A.I., J.E. Sheridan and L.H. Peters. 1992. Survival models of professional staff retention in public accounting firms. *Journal of Managerial Issues*, No. 3, pp. 339-353.

$$ Bartunek, J.M. and C. Reynolds. 1983. Boundary spanning and public accountant role stress. *The Journal of Social Psychology*, October, pp. 65-72.

Bass, B.M. 1990. *Bass & Stogdill's Handbook of Leadership. Theory, Research and Managerial Applications*. The Free Press.

Beard, V. 1994. Accountants in the movies. *Accounting, Organizations and Society*, No. 3, pp. 303-318.

Beattie, V. and Fearnley, S. 1998. Audit market competition: Auditor changes and the impact of tendering. *The British Accounting Review*, September, pp. 261-289.

$$$ Bedeian, A.G., B.G. Burke and R.G. Moffett. 1988. Outcomes of work-family conflict among married male and female professionals. *Journal of Management*, September, pp. 475-491.

Belkaoui, A. 1989. *Behavioral Accounting*. Quorum Books.

Belkaoui, A. and P.D. Picur. 1987. Sources of feedback in a CPA firm. *Journal of Business Finance & Accounting*, Summer, pp. 175-186.

$ Belkaoui, A.R. 1995. Leadership style, dimensions of superior's upward influence and job perception in a public accounting firm: A re-examination of the "Pelz effect". *Accounting and Business Review*, July, pp. 201-216.

Bell, T.B. and A.M. Wright. 1995. *Auditing Practice, Research and Education: A Productive Collaboration*. AICPA.

Benke Jr., R.L. and J.G. Rhode. 1980. The job satisfaction of higher level employees in large certified public accounting firms. *Accounting, Organizations and Society*, No. 2, pp. 187-201.

Benke Jr., R.L. and J.G. Rhode. 1984. Intent to turnover among higher level employees in large CPA firms. *Advances in Accounting*, pp. 157-174.

$$ Bernardi, R.A. 1998. The implications of lifestyle preference on a public accounting career: An exploratory study. *Critical Perspectives on Accounting*, June, pp. 335-351.

$ Bhamornsiri, S. and R.E. Guinn. 1991. The road to partnership in the "big six" firms: Implications for accounting education. *Issues in Accounting Education*, Spring, pp. 9-24.

$$$ Bline, D.M., W.F. Meixner and N. Aranya. 1992. The impact of the work setting on the organizational and professional commitment of accountants. *Research in Governmental and Nonprofit Accounting*, pp. 79-96.

Blocher, E. 1979. Performance effects of different audit staff assignment strategies. *The Accounting Review*, July, pp. 563-573.

Bond, A., J.A. Brierley and M. Tippett. Forthcoming 2001. Analysing quantitative data. In Bond, A. (ed.) *Writing Your Master's Thesis: The Professional Way To Plan, Complete and Present Your Research*.

Boritz, J.E., and D. Cockburn. 1998. Audit symposium panel discussion on assurance services. *Auditing: A Journal of Practice & Theory*, Supplement, pp. 133-151.

Bougen, P.D. 1994. Joking apart: The serious side to the accountant stereotype. *Accounting, Organizations and Society*, No. 3, pp. 319-335.

Bowrin, A.R. 1998. Review and synthesis of audit structure literature. *Journal of Accounting Literature*, pp. 40-71.

$$ Boyer, I. 1995. *The Balance on Trial: Women's Careers in Accountancy*. CIMA.

Brierley, J.A. 1998a. The relationship between accountants' organizational commitment and professional commitment: A meta-analysis. *The Journal of Applied Accounting Research*, March, pp. 35-60.

Brierley, J.A. 1998b. Accountants' organizational-professional conflict: A meta-analysis. *The Journal of Psychology: Interdisciplinary and Applied*, May, pp. 291-300.

Brierley, J.A. 1998c. A meta-analytic review of relationships involving accountants' professional commitment. *Asia-Pacific Journal of Accounting*, June, pp. 45-73.

Brierley, J.A. 1999a. Accountant's job satisfaction: A meta-analysis. *The British Accounting Review*, March, pp. 63-84.

Brierley, J.A. 1999b. A meta-analytic review of the determinants of accountants' organisational turnover intentions. *Accounting and Business Review*, January, pp. 59-83.

Brierley, J.A. 2000a. The organizational commitment of accountants: A meta-analytic examination of its antecedent and consequences. *International Journal of Management*, December, pp. 461-467.

Brierley, J.A. 2000b. An analysis of the impact of the work environment on chartered accountants' professional examination performance. *Journal of Social Psychology*, June, pp. 397-398.

$ Brierley, J.A. and S. Turley. 1995. The organisational turnover intentions of chartered accountants: A test of a causal model. *Accounting and Business Review*, January, pp. 27-54.

Briloff, A.J. 1990. Accountancy and society: A covenant desecrated. *Critical Perspectives on Accounting*, March, pp. 5-30.

$$ Buckley, A. and E. McKenna. 1973. The practising chartered accountant – Job attitudes and professional values. *Accounting and Business Research*, Summer, pp. 197-204.

$$ Bullen, M.L. and E.G. Flamholtz. 1985. A theoretical and empirical investigation of job satisfaction and intended turnover in the large CPA firm. *Accounting, Organizations and Society*, No. 3, pp. 287-302.

$$$ Cao, L.T., S.A. Lynn and B.C. Horn. 1995. The earnings gap between male and female accounting professionals: Empirical evidence and explanations. *Advances in Public Interest Accounting*, pp. 27-50.

$ Carcello, J.V., J.E. Copeland Jr., R.H. Hermanson and D.H. Turner. 1991. A public accounting career: The gap between student expectations and accounting staff experiences. *Accounting Horizons*, September, pp. 1-11.

Charnes, A.K., W.W. Cooper, J.W. Detrick, W.H. Moody and H. Shin. 1990. Optimal hiring decisions for entry-level auditors in a CPA firm: A computerized model for improving hiring practices. *Advances in Accounting*, pp. 247-270.

Choo, F. 1986. Job stress, job performance and auditor personality characteristics. *Auditing: A Journal of Practice & Theory*, Spring, pp. 17-34.

$$$ Choo, F. 1987. Accountants' personality typology and perception of job-related stress: An empirical study. *Accounting and Finance*, November, pp. 13-23.

Choo, F. 1995. Auditors' judgment performance under stress: A test of the predicted relationship by three theoretical models. *Journal of Accounting, Auditing and Finance*, Summer, pp. 611-641.

Chua, W.F. 1986. Radical developments in accounting thought. *The Accounting Review*, October, pp. 601-632.

Ciancanelli, P., S. Gallhofer, C. Humphrey and L. Kirkham. 1990. Gender and accountancy: Some evidence from the UK. *Critical Perspectives on Accounting*, June, pp. 117-144.

$ Coffey, A.J. 1994. 'Timing is everything': Graduate accountants, time and organizational commitment. *Sociology*, November, pp. 943-956.

Cohen, J. 1978. Partialled products are interactions: Partialled powers are curve components. *Psychological Bulletin*, July, pp. 858-866.

Cohen, J. and P. Cohen. 1983. *Applied Multiple Regression/Correlation Analysis for the Behavioral Sciences*, 2nd edition, Lawrence Erlbaum.

$$ Colarelli, S.M., R.A. Dean and C. Konstans. 1987. Comparative effects of personal and situational influences on job outcomes of new professionals. *Journal of Applied Psychology*, August, pp. 558-566.

$$$ Colbert, J.L., K.W. Mossholder and A.G. Bedeian. 1990. Characteristics of professionals in public accounting firms. *Managerial Auditing Journal*, No. 3, pp. 22-24.

$$ Collins, K.M. 1993. Stress and departures from the public accounting profession: A study of gender differences. *Accounting Horizons*, March, pp. 29-38.

$$ Collins, K.M. and L.N. Killough. 1992. An empirical examination of stress in public accounting. *Accounting, Organizations and Society*, No. 6, pp. 535-547.

Collins, S.H. 1988. Blacks in the profession. *Journal of Accountancy*, February, pp. 38, 40-44.

Cousins, J., A. Mitchell, P. Sikka and H. Wilmott. 1998. *Auditors: Holding the Public to Ransom*, Association for Accountancy & Business Affairs.

Coutts, J.A. and J. Roberts. 1995. Segregation: A patriarchal strategy in the professions. *Advances in Public Interest Accounting*, pp. 99-135.

$ Covaleski, M.A., M.W. Dirsmith, J.B. Heian and S. Samuel. 1998. The calculated and the avowed: Techniques of discipline and struggles over identity in big six public accounting firms. *Administrative Science Quarterly*, June, pp. 293-327.

Cowton, C.J. 1999. The relevance of 'irrelevant' research: The case of the research-practice 'gap' in accounting. Mimeo University of Huddersfield.

Cox, D.R. and D. Oakes. 1984. *Analysis of Survival Data*, Chapman and Hill.

Craner, J. and S. Greenfield. 1995. The social, personal and occupational characteristics and attitudes of UK chartered accountants: A functional analysis of the profession. Paper presented to the 1995 European Accounting Association Congress.

$$ Crant, J.M. and T.S. Bateman. 1993. Assignment of credit and blame for performance outcome. *Academy of Management Journal*, March, pp. 7-27.

Crowne, D. and D. Marlowe. 1964. *The Approval Motive: Studies in evaluative dependence*, John Wiley & Sons.

Cushing, B.E. and J.K. Loebbecke. 1986. *Comparison of Audit Methodologies of Large Accounting Firms: Accounting Research Study No. 26*. American Accounting Association.

$ Dalton, D.R., J.W. Hill and R.J. Ramsay. 1997. Women as managers and partners: Context specific predictors of turnover in international public accounting firms. *Auditing: A Journal of Practice & Theory*, Spring, pp. 29-50.

$$$ Daniels, K. and A. Guppy. 1994. Occupational stress social support, job control, and psychological well-being. *Human Relations*, December, pp. 1523-1544.

$ Davidson, R.A. and J.T. Dalby. 1993. Personality profile of female public accountants. *Accounting, Auditing and Accountability Journal*, No.2, pp. 81-97.

$$ Davidson, R.A. and J.T. Dalby. 1993. Personality profiles of Canadian public accountants. *International Journal of Selection and Assessment*, April, pp. 107-116.

$$ Davidson, R.A. and L.D. Etherington. 1995. Personalities of accounting students and public accountants: Implications for accounting educators and the profession. *Journal of Accounting Education*, Fall, pp. 425-444.

$$$ Davy, J.A. and B.R. Stewart. 1995. A comparative study of the antecedents of job dissatisfaction and turnover intentions among

women and men in public accounting firms. *Advances in Public Interest Accounting*, pp. 193-227.

$$$ Day, D.V. and A.G. Bedeian. 1991. Work climate and type A status as predictors of job satisfaction: A test of an interactional perspective. *Journal of Vocational Behavior*, February, pp. 39-52.

$$$ Day, D.V and A.G. Bedeian. 1991. Predicting job performance across organizations: The interaction of work orientation and psychological climate. *Journal of Management*, September, pp. 589-600.

$$ Day, D.V. and S.B. Silverman. 1989. Personality and job performance: Evidence of incremental validity. *Personnel Psychology*, Spring, pp. 25-36.

$$ and $$$ Dean, R.A., K.R. Ferris and C. Konstans. 1988. Occupational reality shock and organizational commitment: Evidence from the accounting profession. *Accounting, Organizations and Society*, No. 3, pp. 235-250.

$$ DeCoster, D.T. and J.G. Rhode. 1971. The accountant's stereotype: Real or imagined, deserved or unwarranted. *The Accounting Review*, October, pp. 651-664.

Dent, J., M. Ezzamel and M. Bourn. 1984. Reflections on research in management accounting and its relationship to practice: An academic view. In Hopwood, A.G. and H. Schreuder (eds.), *European Contributions to Accounting Research: The Achievements of the Last Decade*. Free University Press. pp. 233-253.

$$ Deppe, L.A., J.M. Smith and J.D. Stice. 1992. The debate over post-baccalaureate education: One university's experience. *Issues in Accounting Education*, Spring, pp. 18-36.

Dillard, J.F. 1976. Migration of public accountants into the industrial sector. *Review of Business and Economic Research*, pp. 69-80.

$$ Dillard, J.F. 1979. Applicability of an occupational goal-expectancy model in professional accounting organizations. *Decision Sciences*, April, pp. 161-176.

$$ Dillard, J.F. 1981. An update of the applicability of an occupational goal-expectancy model in professional accounting organizations. *Decision Sciences*, January, pp. 32-38.

$$ Dillard, J.F. and K.R. Ferris. 1979. Sources of professional staff turnover in public accounting firms: Some further evidence. *Accounting, Organizations and Society*, No. 3, pp. 179-186.

Dillard, J.F. and K.R. Ferris. 1989. Individual behavior in professional accounting firms: A review and synthesis. *Journal of Accounting Literature*, pp. 208-234.

$$ Dinius, S.H. and R.B. Rogow. 1988. Application of the delphi method in identifying characteristics big eight firms seek in entry-level accountants. *Journal of Accounting Education*, Spring, pp. 83-101.

Dirsmith, M.W. and M.A. Covaleski. 1985. Informal communications, nonformal communications and mentoring in public accounting. *Accounting, Organizations and Society*, No. 2, pp. 149-169.

$$ Dirsmith, M.W. and M.A. Covaleski. 1985. Practice management issues in public accounting firms. *Journal of Accounting Auditing and Finance*, pp. 5-21.

$ Dirsmith, M.W., J.B. Heian and M.A. Covaleski. 1997. Structure and agency in an institutionalized setting: The application and social transformation of control in the big six. *Accounting, Organizations and Society*, No. 1, pp. 1-27.

$$$ Dodd-McCue, D. and G.B. Wright. 1996. Men, women and attitudinal commitment: The effects of workplace experience and socialization. *Human Relations*, August, pp. 1065-1091.

$$ Dolby, V.J. and R.D. Caplan. 1995. Organizational stress as threat to reputatation: Effects on anxiety at work and at home. *Academy of Management Journal*, December, pp. 1105-1123.

$$ Doucet, M.S., and K.L. Hooks. 1999. Toward an equal future. *Journal of Accountancy*, June, pp. 71-73, 75-76.

Dunnette, M. and W. Barman. 1979. Personnel selection and classification system. *Annual Review of Psychology*, pp. 486-525.

Earnest, K.R., and J.C. Lampe. 1982. Attitudinal differences between male and female auditors. *The Woman CPA*, July, pp.13-16, 18-20.

Earnest, K.R. and J.C. Lampe. 1987. An expectancy theory investigation into causes of employee turnover in public accounting. *Advances in Accounting*, pp. 215-238.

$$ Edwards, J.R., A.J. Baglioni and C.L. Cooper. 1990. Stress, type A, coping, and psychological and physical symptoms: A multi-sample test of alternative models. *Human Relations*, October, pp. 919-956.

Elliott, R.K. 1991. Improvements in the early employment experience. *Accounting Horizons*, September, pp. 114-119.

Elliott, R.K. 1998. Assurance services and the audit heritage. *Auditing: A Journal of Practice & Theory*, Supplement, pp. 1-7.

Ellyson, R.C. and B.C. Shaw. 1970. The psychological assessment and staff recruiting. *Journal of Accountancy*, March, pp. 35-42.

Emby, C. and L.D. Etherington. 1996. Performance evaluation of auditors: Role perceptions of superiors and subordinates. *Auditing: A Journal of Practice & Theory*, Fall, pp. 99-109.

$ Estes, R. 1978. The profession's changing horizons: A survey of practitioners on the present and future importance of selected knowledge and skills. *The International Journal of Accounting*, Spring, pp. 47-70.

$$$ Estes, R. 1984. An intergenerational, comparison of socioeconomic status among CPAs, attorneys, engineers and physicians. *Advances in Accounting*, pp. 3-17.

$$ Farrell, D. and J.C. Peterson. 1984. Commitment, absenteeism, and turnover of new employees: A longitudinal study. *Human Relations*, August. pp. 681-692.

$$ Ferguson, E. and D. Hatherly. 1991. The work environment in the accountancy firm: A comparison of student expectations and trainee expectations. *The British Accounting Review*, June, pp. 123-132.

Ferris, K.R. 1977a. Perceived uncertainty and job satisfaction in the accounting environment. *Accounting, Organizations and Society*, No. 1, pp. 23-28.

Ferris, K.R. 1977b. A test of the expectancy theory of motivation in an accounting environment. *The Accounting Review*, July, pp. 605-615.

Ferris, K.R. 1978. Perceived environmental uncertainty as a mediator of expectancy theory predictions: Some preliminary findings. *Decision Sciences*, July, pp. 379-390.

Ferris, K.R. 1981. Organizational commitment and performance in a professional accounting firm. *Accounting, Organizations and Society*, No. 4, pp. 317-325.

Ferris, K.R. 1982a. Educational predictors of professional pay and performance. *Accounting, Organizations and Society*, No. 3, pp. 225-230.

$ Ferris, K.R. 1982b. Perceived environmental uncertainty, organizational adaptation and employee performance: A longitudinal study in professional accounting firms. *Accounting, Organizations and Society*, No. 1, pp. 13-25.

$ Ferris, K.R. and N. Aranya. 1983. A comparison of two organizational commitment scales. *Personnel Psychology*, pp. 87-98.

Ferris, K.R. and J.F. Dillard. 1988. Individual behavior: Evidence from the accounting environment. In Ferris, K.R. (ed.), *Behavioral Accounting Research: A Critical Analysis*. Century VII Publishing. pp. 281-303.

Ferris, K.R., J.F. Dillard and L. Nethercott. 1980. A comparison of V-I-E model predictions: A cross national study in professional accounting firms. *Accounting, Organizations and Society*, No. 4, pp. 361-368.

Ferris, K.R. and D.F. Larcker. 1983. Explanatory variables of auditor performance in a large public accounting firm. *Accounting, Organizations and Society*, No. 1, pp. 1-11.

Fisher, L. 2000. Is the profession colour blind? *Accountancy*, December, pp. 42-43.

Fisher, R.T. 2001. Role stress, the type A behavior pattern, and external auditor job satisfaction and performance. *Behavioral Research in Accounting*, pp.143-170.

Fogarty, T.J., 1994. Public accounting work experience: The influence of demographic and organizational attributes. *Managerial Auditing Journal.* No. 7. pp. 12-20.

Fogarty, T.J. 1995. Questioning the assumed homogeneity of the behavioral environment of accounting firms: Some exploratory empirical evidence. *The British Accounting Review*, March, pp. 45-59.

Fogarty, T.J., 1996. Gender differences in the perception of the work environment within large international accounting firms. *Managerial Auditing Journal.* No. 2. pp. 10-19.

Fogarty, T.J. 1997. Towards progress in gender research in accounting: Challenges for studies in three domains. *Asia-Pacific Journal of Accounting*, June, pp. 37-58.

$$$ Fogarty, T.J., J. Singh, G.K. Rhoads and R.K. Moore. 2000. Antecedents and consequences of burnout in accounting: Beyond the role stress model. *Behavioural Research in Accounting*, pp 31-67.

Forsyth, D.R. 1980. A taxonomy of ethical ideologies. *Journal of Personality and Social Psychology*, July, pp. 175-184.

Gaertner, J.F. and J.A. Ruhe. 1981. Job-related stress in public accounting. *Journal of Accountancy*, June, pp. 68-74.

$ and $$ Gaffney, M.A., R.A. McEwen and M.J. Welsh. 1993. Gender effects on commitment of public accountants: A test of competing sociological models. *Advances in Public Interest Accounting*, pp. 45-73.

$$$ Gamble, G.O. and M.T. Matteson. 1992. Type A behavior, job satisfaction, and stress among black professionals. *Psychological Reports*, February, pp. 43-50.

$$$ Glover, H.D., P.G. Mynatt and R.G. Schroeder. 2000. The personality, job satisfaction and turnover intentions of African-American male and female-accountants: An examination of the human capital and structural/class theories. *Critical Perspectives on Accounting*, April, pp. 173-192.

$$ Goetz Jr., J.F., P.C. Morrow and J.C. McElroy. 1991. The effect of accounting firm size and member rank on professionalism. *Accounting, Organizations and Society*, No. 2, pp. 159-165.

Goldberg, P. 1978. *Executive Health: How to Recognize Health Danger Signals and Manage Stress Successfully*. McGraw-Hill.

Goss, D. 1995. *Principles of Human Resource Management*, Routledge.

Gouldner, A.W. 1958. Cosmopolitans and locals: Toward an analysis of latent social roles – II. *Administrative Science Quarterly*, March, pp. 444-481.

$$$ Granleese, J. and T.F. Barrett. 1990. The social and personality characteristics of the Irish chartered accountant. *Personality and Individual Differences*, No. 9, pp. 957-964.

$$$ Granleese, J. and T.F. Barrett. 1993. Job satisfaction and the social occupational and personality characteristics of male chartered accountants from three professional bodies. *The British Accounting Review*, June, pp. 177-200.

$$$ Greenhaus, J.H., A.G. Bedeian and K.W Mossholder. 1987. Work experience, job performance and feelings of personal and family well-being. *Journal of Vocational Behavior*, October, pp. 200-215.

$ Greenhaus, J.H., K.M. Collins, R. Singh and S. Parasuraman. 1997. Work and family influence on departure from public accounting. *Journal of Vocational Behavior*, April, pp. 249-270.

$ Gregson, T. 1990a. Communication satisfaction: A path analytic study of accountants affiliated with CPA firms. *Behavioral Research in Accounting*, pp. 32-49.

$ Gregson, T. 1990b. The separate constructs of communication satisfaction and job satisfaction. *Educational and Psychological Measurement*, pp. 39-47.

Gregson, T. 1992a. The advantages of LISREL to accounting researchers. *Accounting Horizons*, December, pp. 42-48.

$$ Gregson, T. 1992b. An investigation of the causal ordering of job satisfaction and organizational commitment in turnover models in accounting. *Behavioral Research in Accounting*, pp. 80-95.

$ Gregson, T. and D.M. Bline. 1989. The relationship of communication satisfaction to turnover intentions and job satisfaction for Certified Public Accountants. *Advances in Accounting*, pp. 203-222.

$$ Gregson, T., J. Wendell and J. Aono. 1994. Role ambiguity, role conflict and perceived environmental uncertainty: Are the scales measuring separate constructs for accountants? *Behavioral Research in Accounting*, pp. 144-159.

$$ Groves, R., M. Poole and P. Broder. 1984. Professional commitment of the practising chartered accountant in modern Britain. *Accounting and Business Research*, Autumn, pp. 319-331.

Gwilliam, D. 1987. *A Survey of Auditing Research*. ICAEW/Prentice-Hall.

Gwilliam, D. 1995. Auditing research – Unfulfilled aspirations? University of Wales, Aberystwyth Working Paper.

Habermas, J. 1978. *Knowledge and Human Interest*, 2nd edition, Heinemann.

$$ Hakel, M.D., T.D. Hollmann and M.D. Dunnette. 1970. Accuracy of interviewers, certified public accoutants, and students in identifying the interests of accountants. *Journal of Applied Psychology*, April, pp. 115-119.

Hammond, T.D. 1997. From complete exclusion to minimal inclusion: African Americans and the public accounting industry, 1965-1988. *Accounting, Organizations and Society*, No. 1, pp. 29-53.

Hammond, T.D. and D.W. Streeter. 1994. Overcoming, barriers: Early African-American certified public accountants. *Accounting, Organizations and Society*, No. 3, pp. 271-288.

$$ Hammond, T.D. and K. Paige. 1999. Still seeking the ideal. *Journal of Accountancy*, September, pp. 75-77, 79.

Harrell, A. 1990. A longitudinal examination of large CPA firms auditors' personnel turnover. *Advances in Accounting*, pp. 233-246.

Harrell, A., E. Chewing and M. Taylor. 1986. Organizational-professional conflict and the job satisfaction and turnover intentions of internal auditors. *Auditing: A Journal of Practice & Theory*, Spring, pp. 109-121.

Harrell, A. and R. Eickhoff. 1988. Auditors' influence-orientation and their affective responses to the "big eight" work environment. *Auditing: A Journal of Practice & Theory*, Spring, pp. 105-118.

Harrell, A. and M. Stahl. 1981. A behavioural decision theory approach for measuring McClelland's trichotomy of needs. *Journal of Applied Psychology*, April, pp. 242-247.

$ Harrell, A.M. and M.J. Stahl. 1984. McClelland's trichotomy of needs theory and the job satisfaction and work performance of CPA firm professionals. *Accounting, Organizations and Society*, No. 3/4, pp. 241-252.

Harrell, A. and A. Wright. 1990. Empirical evidence on the validity and reliability of behaviorally anchored rating scales for auditors. *Auditing: A Journal of Practice & Theory*, Fall, pp. 134-149.

Haskins, M.E., A.L. Baglioni Jr. and C.L. Cooper. 1987. An investigation of the sources, moderators, and psychological symptoms of stress among audit seniors. *Contemporary Accounting Research*, No. 2, pp. 361-385.

$$ Hassell, J.M. and H.W. Hennessey Jr. 1989. An examination of factors important in the CPA recruiting process. *Journal of Accounting Education*, Fall, pp. 217-231.

$$ Hassell, J.M., H.W. Hennessey Jr. and J.E. Rebele. 1992. A reexamination of the relative importance of CPA firms' performance evaluation criteria. *Advances in Accounting*, pp. 121-142.

Hawksley, F. 1995. Wanted! Newly qualifieds. *Accountancy*, October, pp. 42-44.

$$ Hellriegel, D. and G.E. White. 1973. Turnover of professionals in public accounting: A comparative analysis. *Personnel Psychology*, Summer, pp. 239-249.

Hermanson, R.H., J.V. Carcello, D.R. Hermanson, B.J. Milano, G.A. Polansky and D.Z. Williams. 1995. Better environment, better staff. *Journal of Accountancy*, April, pp. 39-43.

$$ Hill, A.P. and R.M.S. Wilson. 1994. The impact of professional commitment on early career success in accounting firms. *International Journal of Selection and Assessment*, October, pp. 249-254.

Hood, J.N. and C.S. Koberg. 1991. Accounting firm cultures and creativity among accountants. *Accounting Horizons*, September, pp. 12-19.

Hooks, K.L. 1992. Gender effects and labour supply in public accounting: An agenda of research issues. *Accounting, Organizations and Society*, No. 3/4, pp. 343-366.

$ Hooks, K.L., P.B. Thomas and W.D. Stout. 1997. Retention of women in public accounting: Directions for future research. *Advances in Accounting*, pp. 17-48.

Hoppock, R. 1935. *Job Satisfaction*. Harper and Row.

Hopwood, A.G. 1988. Accounting Research and Accounting Practice: The Ambiguous Relationship Between the Two. Deloitte Haskins & Sells Lecture, University of Wales, Aberystwyth.

House, R. and J. Rizzo. 1972. Role conflict and ambiguity as critical variables in a model of organizational behavior. *Organizational Behavior and Human Performance*, June, pp. 467-505.

Hull, R.P. and P.H. Umansky. 1997. An examination of gender stereotyping as an explanation for vertical job segregation in public accounting. *Accounting, Organizations and Society*. No. 6, pp. 507-528.

Hunt, S.C. 1995. A review and synthesis of research in performance evaluation in public accounting. *Journal of Accounting Literature*, pp. 107-139.

Hyatt, T.A. and D.F. Prawitt. 2001. Does congruence between audit structure and auditors' locus control affect job performance? *The Accounting Review*, April, pp.263-274.

ICAEW. 2000. *Education, Training and Student Salary Statistics 1998/99*. ICAEW.

$$$ Imada, A.S., C. Fletcher and A. Dalessio. 1980. Individual correlates of an occupational stereotype: A reexamination of the stereotype of accountants. *Journal of Applied Psychology*, August, pp. 436-439.

Ivancevich, J.M. and M.T. Matteson. 1988. Type A behavior and the healthy individual. *British Journal of Medical Psychology*, pp. 37-56.

$ Iyer, V.M., E.M. Bamber and R.M. Barefield. 1997. Identification of accounting firm alumni with their former firm: Antecedents and outcomes. *Accounting, Organizations and Society*, No. 3/4, pp. 315-336.

$$ Jackofsky, E.F., K.R. Ferris and B.G. Breckenridge. 1986. Evidence for a curvilinear relationship between job performance and turnover. *Journal of Management*, Spring, pp. 105-111.

$$ Jeffrey, C. and N. Weatherholt. 1994. Accountants' attitudes toward professionalism: USA versus Taiwan and Korea. *Asia-Pacific Journal of Accounting*, December, pp. 61-72.

$$ Jeffrey, C. and N. Weatherholt. 1996. Ethical development, professional commitment and rule observance attitudes: A study of CPAs and corporate accountants. *Behavioral Research in Accounting*, pp. 8-31.

Jeffrey, C., N. Weatherholt and S. Lo. 1996. Ethical development, professional commitment and rule observance attitudes: A study of auditors in Taiwan. *The International Journal of Accounting*, No. 3, pp. 365-379.

Jeppesen, K.K. 1998. Reinventing auditing, redefining consulting and independence. *European Accounting Review*, September, pp. 517-539.

Jiambalvo, J. 1979. Performance evaluation and directed job effort: Model development and analysis in a CPA firm setting. *Journal of Accounting Research*, Autumn, pp. 436-455.

Jiambalvo, J. 1982. Measures of accuracy and congruence in the performance evaluation of CPA personnel: Replication and extension. *Journal of Accounting Research*, Spring, pp. 152-161.

Jiambalvo, J. and J. Pratt. 1982. Task complexity and leadership effectiveness in CPA firms. *The Accounting Review*, October, pp. 734-750.

Jiambalvo, J., D.J.H. Watson and J.V. Baumler. 1983. An examination of performance evaluation decisions in CPA firm subunits. *Accounting, Organizations and Society*, No. 1, pp. 13-29.

Johnson, E.N., D.J. Lowe and P.M.J. Reckers. 1996. An examination of direct and indirect gender effects in public accounting. *Advances in Accounting*, pp. 179-192.

Jones, E. 1995. *True and Fair: A History of Price Waterhouse*. Hamish Hamilton.

Joreskog, K. and D. Sorbom. 1993. *LISREL 8: User's Guide*. Scientific Software.

Kahn, R.L. P.M. Wolfe, R.P. Quinn, J.E. Snoek and R.A. Rosenthal. 1964. *Organizational Stress: Studies in Role Conflict and Role Ambiguity*. John Wiley.

Kaplan, S.E. and P.M.J. Reckers. 1985. An examination of auditor performance evaluation. *The Accounting Review*, July, pp. 477-487.

Kaplan, S.E. and P.M.J. Reckers. 1991. An attributional analysis of the performance evaluation process. *Advances in Accounting*, pp. 227-248.

Kaplan. S.E. and P.M.J. Reckers. 1993. An examination of the effects of accountability tactics on performance evaluation judgements in public accounting. *Behavioral Research in Accounting*, pp. 101-123.

Kaplan, S.E., A.K. Keinath and J.C. Walo. 2001. An examination of perceived barriers to mentoring in public accounting. *Behavioral Research in Accounting*, pp. 195-220.

Kaplan, S.E., A.K. Keinath and J.C. Walo. 1999/2000. Do peers supplement or substitute for mentors in public accounting? *Accounting Enquiries*, Fall/Winter, pp. 129-176.

Kelley, H.H. 1973. The process of causal attribution. *American Psychologist*, February, pp. 107-128.

Kelley, H.H. and J.L. Michela. 1980. Attribution theory and research. *Annual Review of Psychology*, pp. 457-501.

Kelley, T. and L. Margheim. 1990. The impact of time budget pressure, personality, and leadership variables on dysfunctional auditor behavior. *Auditing: A Journal of Practice & Theory*, Spring, pp. 21-42.

$$ Kemey, E.R., A.G. Bedeian, K.W. Mossholder and J. Touliatos. Outcomes of role stress: Multisample constructive replication. *Academy of Management Journal*, June, pp. 363-375.

$ Ketchand, A.A. and J.R. Strawser. 1998. The existence of multiple measures of organizational commitment and experience-related differences in a public accounting setting. *Behavioral Research in Accounting*, pp. 109-137.

Ketchand, A.A. and J.R. Strawser. 2001. Multiple dimensions of organizational commitment: Implications for future accounting research. *Behavioral Research in Accounting*, pp. 221-251.

Kida, T.E. 1984. Performance evaluation and review meeting characteristics in public accounting firms. *Accounting, Organizations and Society*, No. 2, pp. 137-147.

Kinney Jr., W.R. 1986. Audit technology and preference for auditing standards. *Journal of Accounting and Economics*, March, pp. 73-89.

Kirkham, L.M. 1992. Integrating herstory and history in accounting. *Accounting, Organizations and Society*, No. 3/4, pp. 287-297.

Kirkham, L.M. and A. Loft. 1993. Gender and the construction of the professional accountant. *Accounting, Organizations and Society*, No. 6, pp. 507-558.

$$ Knapp, C. 1980. Examining the turnover problem. *Journal of Accountancy*, November, p. 86 & 88.

$$ Knapp, M.C. and S. Kwon. 1991. Toward a better understanding of the underrepresentation of women and minorities in big eight firms. *Advances in Public Interest Accounting*, pp. 47-62.

Kopelman, R.E. 1983. Across individual, within individual and return on effort versions of expectancy theory. *Organizational Behavior and Human Performance*, October, pp. 124-143.

Kram, K.E. 1985. *Mentoring at Work: Developmental Relationships in Organizational Life*. Scott Foresman & Co.

Kram, K.E. and L.A. Isabella. 1985. Mentoring Alternatives: The Role of Peer Relationships in Career Development, *Academy of Management Journal*, March, pp.110-132.

Kroeger, O. and J. Thuesen. 1992. *Type Talk at Work*. Bantam-Doubleday.

Kwok, W.C.C., and D.J. Sharp. 1998. A review of construct measurement issues in behavioural accounting research. *Journal of Accounting Literature*, pp. 137-174.

$$ Lachman, R. and N. Aranya. 1986a. Job attitudes and turnover intentions among professionals in different work settings. *Organization Studies*, No. 3, pp. 279-293.

$$$ Lachman, R. and N. Aranya. 1986b. Evaluation of alternative models of commitments and job attitudes of professionals. *Journal of Occupational Behavior*, pp. 227-243.

Larson, M.S. 1977. *The Rise of Professionalism: A Sociological Analysis*. University of California Press.

Lee, T. 1995. Shaping the US academic accounting research profession: The American accounting association and the social construction of a professional elite. *Critical Perspectives on Accounting*, June, pp. 241-261.

$$$ Lee, T.W., T.R. Mitchell, B.C. Holtom, L.S. McDaniel and J.W. Hill. 1999. The unfolding model of voluntary turnover: A replication and extension. *Academy of Managerial Journal*, August, pp. 450-462.

Lehman, C.R. 1992. Herstory in accounting: The first eighty years. *Accounting, Organizations and Society*, No. 3/4, pp. 261-285.

$$ Lengermann, J.J. 1971. Supposed and actual differences in professional autonomy among CPAs as related to type of work organization and size of firm. *The Accounting Review*, October, pp. 665-675.

Lindsay, R.M. 1995. Reconsidering the status of tests of significance: An alternative criterion of adequacy. *Accounting, Organizations and Society*, No. 1, pp. 35-53.

Litwin, M.S. 1995. *How to Measure Survey Reliability and Validity*. Sage.

Locke, E.A. 1976. The nature and causes of job satisfaction. In Dunnette, M. (ed.), *Handbook of Industrial and Organizational Psychology*, Rand McNally, pp. 1297-1319.

$ Loeb, S.E. and M.J. Gannon. 1971. Need satisfaction and staff retention in large certified public accounting firms. *The CPA Journal*, April, pp. 327-329.

Lowe, D.J., P.M. Reckers and D. Sanders. 2001. The influence of gender, ethnicity, and individual differences on perceptions of career progression in public accounting. *International Journal of Auditing*, March, pp. 53-71.

$$$ Lynn, S.A., L.T. Cao and B.C. Horn. 1996. The influence of career stage on the work attitudes of male and female accounting professionals. *Journal of Organizational Behavior*, March, pp. 135-149.

Macdonald, K.M. 1995. *The Sociology of the Professions*. Sage.

$ Maher, M.W., K.V. Ramanathan and R.B. Peterson. 1979. Preference congruency, information accuracy and employee performance: A field study. *Journal of Accounting Research*, Autumn, pp. 476-503.

$ Marxen, D.E. 1996. The Big 6 experience: A retrospective account by alumni. *Accounting Horizons*, June, pp. 73-87.

Matteson, M.T. and J.M. Ivancevich. 1982. *Managing Job Stress and Health*. The Free Press.

Matteson, M.T., J.M. Ivancevich and S.V. Smith. 1984. Relation of Type A behavior to performance and satisfaction among sales personnel. *Journal of Vocational Behavior*, October, pp. 203-214.

Maupin, R.J. 1990. Sex role identity and career success of certified public accountants. *Advances in Public Interest Accounting*, pp. 97-105.

Maupin, R.J. 1993. Why are there so few women accounting partners? Male and female accountants disagree. *Managerial Auditing Journal*, No. 5, pp. 10-18.

Maupin, R.J. and C.R. Lehman. 1994. Talking heads: Stereotypes, status, sex roles and satisfaction of females and male auditors. *Accounting, Organizations and Society*, No. 4/5, pp. 427-437.

McClelland, D.C. and R.E. Boyatzis. 1982. Leadership motive and long-term success in management. *Journal of Applied Psychology*, December, pp. 737-743.

McGregor Jr., C.C., L. Killough and R.Brown. 1989. An investigation of organizational-professional conflict in management accounting. *Journal of Management Accounting Research*, pp. 104-118.

Meixner, W.F. and D.M. Bline. 1989. Professional and job-related attitudes and behaviors they influence among governmental accountants. *Accounting, Auditing & Accountability Journal*, No. 1, pp. 8-20.

Meuwissen, R.H.G. 1998. Career advancement in audit firms: an empirical study of university-educated and non university-educated Dutch auditors. *Accounting Education: An International Journal*, March, pp. 35-50.

Michaelson, L.K. 1973. Leader organisation, leader behavior, group effectiveness and situational favorability: An empirical extension of the contingency model. *Organizational Behavior and Human Performance*, April, pp. 226-245.

Mitchell, B.N. and V. L. Flintall. 1990. The status of the black CPA: Twenty year update. *Journal of Accountancy*, August, pp. 59-61, 63, 65, 67, 69.

$$$ Mitchell, V.F. and P. Moudgill. 1976. Measurement of Maslow's need hierarchy. *Organizational Behavior and Human Performance*, August, pp. 334-349.

$ Moizer, P. and J, Pratt. 1988. The evaluation of performance in firms of chartered accountants. *Accounting and Business Research*, Summer, pp. 227-237.

Montagna, P.D. 1974. *Certified Public Accounting: A Sociological View of a Profession in Change*. Scholars.

Morrison, E.W. 1993a. Newcomer information seeking: Exploring types, modes, sources, and outcomes. *Academy of Management Journal*, September, pp. 557-589.

Morrison, E.W. 1993b. Longitudinal study of the effects of information seeking on newcomer socialization. *Journal of Applied Psychology*, April, pp. 173-183.

$$ Morrow, P.C. and J.C. Goetz Jr. 1988. Professionalism as a form of work commitment. *Journal of Vocational Behavior*, February, pp. 92-111.

$$ Mossholder, K.W., A.G. Bedian, J. Touliatos and A.I. Barkman. 1985. An examination of intraoccupational differences: Personality perceived work climate, and outcome preferences. *Journal of Vocational Behavior*, April, pp. 164-176.

$$$ Moyes, G.D., I. Hasan and F.R. Wulsin. 1999. Certified public accountant and compensation: An empirical analysis. *International Journal of Auditing,* November, pp. 207-223.

$$$ Moyes, G.D., P.A. Williams and B.Z. Quigley. 2000. The relation between perceived treatment discrimination and job satisfaction among African-American accounting professionals. *Accounting Horizons*, August, pp. 21-48.

Murray, D. and K.B. Frazier. 1986. A within-subjects test of expectancy theory in a public accounting environment. *Journal of Accounting Research,* Autumn, pp. 400-404.

$$$ Mynatt, P.G., J.S. Omundson, R.G. Schroeder and M.B. Stevens. 1997. The impact of Anglo and Hispanic ethnicity, gender, position,

personality and job satisfaction on turnover intentions: A path analytic investigation. *Critical Perspectives on Accounting*, December, pp. 657-683.

Nemeroff, W. and K. Wexley. 1979. An exploration of the relationship between performance feedback interview characteristics and interview outcomes as perceived by managers and subordinates. *Journal of Occupational Psychology*, March, pp. 25-34.

$$ Nichols, D., R.K. Robinson, B.J. Reithel and G.M. Franklin. 1997. An exploratory study of sexual behavior in accounting firms: Do male and female CPAs interpret sexual harassment differently? *Critical Perspectives on Accounting*, June, pp. 249-264.

$ Norris, D.R. and R.E. Niebuhr. 1984. Professionalism, organizational commitment and job satisfaction in an accounting organization. *Accounting, Organizations and Society*. No. 1, pp. 49-59.

$ O'Driscoll, M.P. and T.A. Beehr. 1994. Supervising behaviors, role stressors and uncertainty as predictors of personal outcomes for subordinates. *Journal of Organizational Behavior*, March, pp. 141-155.

$$$ Olson, J.E. and I.H. Frieze. 1986. Women accountants – Do they earn as much as men? *Management Accounting* (USA), June, pp. 27-31.

Otley, D.T. and B.J. Pierce. 1995. The control problem in public accounting firms: An empirical study of the impact of leadership style. *Accounting, Organizations and Society*, No. 5, pp. 405-420.

$ and $$ Page, M.J., B.E. Elliott and N.S. Bristow. 1989. *Staffing and the Smaller Firm*. ICAEW.

$$$ Paresuraman, S., J.H. Greenhaus, S. Rabinowitz, A.G. Bedeian and K.W. Mossholder. 1989. Work and family variables as mediators of the relationship between wives' employment and husbands' well-being. *Academy of Management Journal*, March, pp. 185-201.

Parker, L.D., K.R. Ferris and D.T. Otley. 1989. *Accounting for the Human Factor*. Prentice Hall.

Parker, R.H. 1986. *The Development of the Accountancy Profession in Britain to the Early Twentieth Century*. Academy of Accounting Historians.

$$ Pasewark, W.R. and J.R. Strawser. 1996. The determinants and outcomes associated with job insecurity in a professional accounting environment. *Behavioral Research in Accounting*, pp. 91-113.

Pasewark,W.R., J.R. Strawser and J.E. Wilkerson. 1994. An empirical examination of the relationships among leader behaviors, audit team performance and staff satisfaction. *Advances in Accounting*, pp. 143-166.

$ Pearson, D.A., S.H. Westcott and R.E. Seiler. 1985. A comparative study of stress in public accounting: Differences between men and women. *The Woman CPA*, July, pp. 16-18.

Perrin, S. 1997. Spot the difference: How do graduates choose a big six firm? *Accountancy*, October, pp. 50-51.

Pillsbury, C., L. Capozzoli and A. Ciampa. 1989. A synthesis of research studies regarding the upward mobility of women in public accounting. *Accounting Horizons*, March, pp. 63-70.

Porter, L.W., R.M. Steers, R.T. Mowday and P.V. Boulain. 1974. Organizational commitment, job satisfaction and turnover among psychiatric technicians. *Journal of Applied Psychology*, October, pp. 603-609.

Power, M. 1994. *The Audit Explosion*. Demos.

Power, M. 1997. *The Audit Society: Rituals of Verification*. Oxford University Press.

$$ Poznanski, P.J. and D.M. Bline. 1997. Using structural equation modeling to investigate the causal ordering of job satisfaction and organizational commitment among staff accountants. *Behavioral Research in Accounting*, pp. 154-171.

$ Pratt, J. and P. Beaulieu. 1992. Organizational culture in public accounting: Size, technology, rank and functional area. *Accounting, Organizations and Society*, No. 7, pp. 667-684.

Pratt, J. and J. Jiambalvo. 1981. Relationships between leader behaviors and audit team performance. *Accounting, Organizations and Society*, No. 2, pp. 133-142.

Pratt, J. and J. Jiambalvo. 1982. Determinants of leader behavior in an audit environment. *Accounting, Organizations and Society*, No. 4, pp. 369-379.

$$ Pratt, J., L.C. Mohrweis and P. Beaulieu. 1993. The interaction between national and organizational culture in accounting firms: An extension. *Accounting, Organizations and Society*, No. 7/8, pp. 621-628.

Previts, G.J. 1985. *The Scope of CPA Services – a Study of the Development of the Concept of Independence and the Profession's Role in Society*. Wiley.

PricewaterhouseCoopers, 1998. *Human Resource Business Briefing*, October.

Purvis, S.E. and R.L. Panich. 1986. Improving the first-year retention rate of entry-level professionals. *CPA Journal*, December, pp. 101-103.

$$ Ramanathan, K.V., R.B. Peterson and M.W. Maher. 1976. Strategic goals and performance criteria in CPA firms. *Journal of Accountancy*, January, pp. 56-64.

Ramsay, R. 1994. Senior/manager differences in audit workpaper review performances. *Journal of Accounting Research*, Spring, pp. 127-135.
Rasch, R.H. and A. Harrell. 1990. The impact of personal characteristics on the turnover behavior of accounting professionals. *Auditing: A Journal of Practice & Theory*, Spring, pp. 90-102.
Rebele, J.E. and R.E. Michaels. 1990. Independent auditors' role stress: Antecedent, outcome and moderating variables. *Behavioral Research in Accounting*, pp. 124-153.
Rebele, J.E., R.E. Michaels and R. Wachter. 1996. The relationship of career stage to job outcomes and role stress: A study of external auditors. *Advances in Accounting*, pp. 241-258.
$$$ Reed, S.A. and S.H. Kratchman. 1990. The effects of changing role requirements on accountants. *Advances in Public Interest Accounting*, pp. 107-136.
$$$ Reed, S.A., S.H. Kratchman and R.H. Strawser. 1994. Job satisfaction, organizational commitment and turnover intentions of United States accountants: The impact of locus of control and gender. *Accounting, Auditing and Accountability Journal*, No. 1, pp. 31-58.
$$$ Reed Accountancy. 1996. The Anatomy of the 90's Accountant. A Major Survey into the Attitudes and Lifestyle of Accountants Today. Reed Accountancy.
Regel, R.W. and D. Murray. 1989. Staff performance evaluation by auditors: The effects of training on accuracy and consensus. *Advances in Accounting*, pp. 223-239.
$$ Rentsch, J.R. 1990. Climate and culture: Interaction and qualitative differences in organizational meanings. *Journal of Applied Psychology*, December, pp. 668-681.
$$ Rhode, J.G., J.E. Sorensen and E.E. Lawler III. 1976. An analysis of personal characteristics related to professional staff turnover in public accounting firms. *Decision Sciences*, October, pp. 771-800.
$$ Rhode, J.G., J.E. Sorensen and E.E. Lawler III. 1977. Sources of professional staff turnover in public accounting firms revealed by exit interview. *Accounting, Organizations and Society*, No. 2, pp. 165-175.
$$ Riordan, D.A. and Street, D.L. 1998. Predicting stress in the public accounting environment: A revised approach based on the medical literature. *Accounting Enquiries*, February, pp. 275-312.
Rizzo, J., R. House and S. Litzman. 1970. Role conflict and ambiguity in complex organizations. *Administrative Science Quarterly*, June, pp. 150-163.
Robson, G.S., D.R. Wholey and R.M. Barefield. 1996. Institutional determinants of individual mobility: Bringing the profession back in. *Academy of Management Journal*, June, pp. 397-420.

Ross, J. and K.R. Ferris. 1981. Interpersonal attraction and organizational outcomes: A field examination. *Administrative Science Quarterly*, December, pp. 617-632.

Rotter, J.B. 1966. Generalized expectancies for internal versus external control of reinforcement. *Psychological Monographs* No. 1.

$$ Saks, A.M. 1996. The relationship between the amount and helpfulness of entry training and work outcomes. *Human Relations*, April, pp. 429-451.

$ Saks, A.M. and D.A. Waldman. 1998. The relationship between age and job performance evaluations for entry-level professionals. *Journal of Organizational Behavior*, July, pp. 409-419.

Sales, S.M. 1969. Differences among individuals in affective, behavioral, biochemical and physiological responses to variations in workload. Dissertation Abstracts International, 30, 2407B University Microfilms No. 69-18098.

$$ and $$$ Scandura, T.A. and B.R. Ragins. 1993. The effects of sex and gender role orientation mentorship in male-dominated occupations. *Journal of Vocational Behavior*, December, pp. 251-256.

$$ Scandura, T.A. and R.E. Viator. 1994. Mentoring in public accounting firms: An analysis of mentor-protégé relationships, mentorship functions, and protégé turnover intentions. *Accounting, Organizations and Society*, No. 8, pp. 717-734.

$$$ Schaefer, J. and M. Zimmer. 1995. Gender and earnings of certain accountants and auditors: A comparative study of industries and regions. *Journal of Accounting and Public Policy*, Winter, pp. 265-291.

$$ Schell, B.H. and V.M. DeLuca. 1991. Task-achievement, obsessive-compliance, type A traits, and job satisfaction of professionals in public practice accounting. *Psychological Reports*, pp. 611-630.

Schepanski, A., R.M. Tubbs and R.A. Grimlund. 1992. Issues of concern regarding within- and between- subjects designs in behavioral accounting research. *Journal of Accounting Literature*, pp. 121-150.

$ Schloemer, P.G. and M.S. Schloemer. 1997. The personality types and preferences of CPA firm professionals: An analysis of changes in the profession. *Accounting Horizons*, December, pp. 24-39.

$$ Schroeder, R.G., J.M. Cathey, A. Reinstein and B.N. Schwartz. 1993. Organizational-professional commitment and central life interests of public accountants: A firm size and level of authority analysis. *Accounting Enquiries*, February, pp. 405-442.

$$ Schroeder, R.G. and L.F. Imdieke. 1977. Local-cosmopolitan and bureaucratic perceptions in public accounting firms. *Accounting, Oranizations and Society*, No. 1, pp. 39-45.

Schroeder, R.G., A. Reinstein and B.N. Schwartz. 1992. The impact of audit technology on organizational-professional commitment in large public accounting firms. *Advances in Accounting*, pp. 175-195.

Senatra, P.T. 1980. Role conflict, role ambiguity and organizational climate in a public accounting firm. *The Accounting Review*, October, pp. 594-603.

Senatra, P. 1988. What are the sources and consequences of stress? Do men and women differ in their perceptions? *The Women CPA*, July, pp. 13-16.

Shaub, M.K., D.W. Finn and P. Munter. 1993. The effects of auditors' ethical orientation on commitment and ethical sensitivity. *Behavioral Research in Accounting*, pp. 145-169.

Shephard, L.R. 1961. Orientation of scientists and engineers. *Pacific Sociological Review*, Fall, pp. 79-83.

$ Sheridan, J.E. 1992. Organizational culture and employee retention. *Academy of Management Journal*, December, pp. 1036-1056.

Siegel, P.H. 1987. Auditor performance and educational preparation: An analysis. *Issues in Accounting Education*, Spring, pp. 127-140.

Siegel, P.H., M.M. Blank and J.T. Rigsby. 1991. Socialisation of the accounting professional: Evidence of the effect of educational structure on subsequent auditor retention and advancement. *Accounting, Auditing & Accountability Journal*, No. 4, pp. 58-70.

$$ Siegel, P.H., A. Reinstein, K.E. Karim & J.T. Rigsby. 1998. The role of peer relationships during CPA firm mergers. *Behavioral Research in Accounting*, (Supplement), pp. 270-277.

Siegel, P.H. and J.T. Rigsby. 1988. The relationship of accounting internships and subsequent professional performance. *Issues in Accounting Education*, Fall, pp. 423-432.

Siegel, P.H., J.T. Rigsby, S.P. Agrawal and J.R. Leavins. 1995. Auditor professional performance and the mentor relationship within the public accounting firm. *Accounting, Auditing & Accountability Journal*, No. 4, pp. 3-22.

Siegel, P.H., J.T. Rigsby and J. Leavins. 1992. An analysis of the relative contributions of experience/education to the professional development of auditors. *Advances in Accounting*, pp. 143-158.

Siegel, P.H. and J.D. Spiceland. 1988. The effect of educational background on auditor success. *The Accounting Educators' Journal*, Spring, pp. 22-28.

$ Silverstone, R. and A. Williams. 1979. Recruitment, training, employment and careers of women chartered accountants in England and Wales. *Accounting and Business Research*, Spring, pp. 105-121.

$$ Smith, K.J., J.A. Davy and G.S. Everly Jr. 1995. An examination of the antecedents of job dissatisfaction and turnover intentions among CPAs in public accounting. *Accounting Enquiries*, August, pp. 99-142.

$$$ Smith, K.J., G.S. Everly Jr. and T.R. Johns. 1993. The role stress arousal in the dynamics of the stressor-to-illness process among accountants. *Contemporary Accounting Research*, Spring, pp. 432-449.

Snead, K. and A. Harrell. 1991. The impact of psychological factors on the job satisfaction of senior auditors. *Behavioral Research in Accounting*, pp. 85-96.

$ Soeters, J. and H. Schreuder. 1988. The interaction between national and organizational cultures in accounting firms. *Accounting, Organizations and Society*, No. 1, pp. 75-85.

Sorensen, J.E. 1967. Professional and bureaucratic organization in the public accounting firm. *The Accounting Review*, July, pp. 553-565.

$$ Sorensen, J.E., J.G. Rhode and E.E. Lawler III. 1973. The generation gap in public accounting. *Journal of Accountancy*, December, pp. 42-50.

$$ Sorensen, J.E. and T.L. Sorensen. 1974. The conflict of professionals in bureaucratic organizations. *Administrative Science Quarterly*, March, pp. 98-106.

Spiceland, J.D., P.H. Siegel and C.R. George. 1992. Educational preparation of auditors, promotion time and turnover: A survival analysis. *Advances in Accounting*, pp. 61-76.

Stahl, M. and A. Harrell. 1981. Modelling effort decisions with behavioral decision theory: Toward an individual differences model of expectancy theory. *Organizational Behavior and Human Performance*, pp. 303-325.

$$ Stahl, M.J. and A.M. Harrell. 1982. Evolution and validation of a behavioral decision theory measurement approach to achievement, power and affiliation. *Journal of Applied Psychology*, December, pp. 744-751.

Stark, A. and M. Walker. 1998. The determinants of success in the examinations of the Institute of Chartered Accountants in England and Wales: A Preliminary Analysis of the ICAEW Archive. Unpublished working paper, University of Manchester.

Steel, C.G. 1976. Discussants' response to Sorensen, J.E., T. Sorensen, J. Rhode and E. Lawler. A behavioral study of staff retention in the public accounting profession. *Symposium on Auditing Research 1974*, University of Illinois – Champaign.

Steele, A. 1983. The market for publicly subsidised research in auditing: A UK perspective. Paper presented to the Auditing Research Conference, University of Manchester.

$ and $$$ Street, D.L. and A.C. Bishop. 1991. An empirical examination of the need profiles of professional accountants. *Behavioral Research in Accounting*, pp. 97-116.

Street, D.L., R.G. Schroeder and B. Schwartz. 1993. The central life interests and organizational professional commitment of men and women employed by public accounting firms. *Advances in Public Interest Accounting*, pp. 201-229.

Stevens, M. 1991. *The Big Six: Selling Out of America's Top Accounting Firms*. Simon Schuster.

Super, D.E. 1957. *The Psychology of Careers*. Harper and Brothers.

Swanson, Z.L. and N.J. Gross. 1998. A comparison of academics', practitioners' and users' perspectives toward the research of accounting practice. *Critical Perspectives on Accounting*, August, pp. 467-485.

$$ Thomas, P.B. 1991. Role conflicts in public accounting: Can individual vigilance suffice? *Advances in Public Interest Accounting*, pp. 63-82.

$ Trapp, M.W., R.H. Hermanson and D.H. Turner. 1989. Current perceptions of issues related to women employed in public accounting. *Accounting Horizons*, March, pp. 71-85.

Trotman, K.T. 1998. Audit judgment research - Issues addressed, research methods and future directions. *Accounting and Finance*, November, pp. 115-156.

$$ Trump, G.W. and H.S. Hendrickson. 1971. Staff retention in public accounting firms. *Journal of Accountancy*, January, pp. 87-90.

Turley, S. and M. Cooper. 1991. *Auditing in the United Kingdom – A Study of the Development in the Audit Methodologies of Large Accounting Firms*. Prentice Hall.

Tyra, A. 1980. Staff turnover in CPA firms. *The Women CPA*, January, pp. 13-28.

$$ Viator, R.E. 1999. An analysis of formal mentoring programs and perceived barriers to obtaining a mentor at large public accounting firms. *Accounting Horizons*, March, pp. 37-53.

$ Viator, R.E. 2001a. The association of formal and informal public accounting mentoring with role stress and related job outcomes. *Accounting, Organizations and Society*, January, pp. 73-93.

$$$ Viator, R.E. 2001b. An examination of African-Americans access to public accounting mentors: perceived barriers and intentions to leave. *Accounting, Organizations and Society*, August, pp. 541-561.

$$ Viator, R.E. and T.A. Scandura. 1991. A study of mentor-protégé relationships in large public accounting firms. *Accounting Horizons*, September, pp. 20-30.

Vroom, H. 1964. *Work and Motivation*. John Wiley & Sons.

Wanous, J.P. and E.E. Lawler. 1972. Measurement and meaning of job satisfaction. *Journal of Applied Psychology*, April, pp. 259-273.

$$ White, G.E. and D. Hellriegel. 1973. Attitudes of CPAs related to professional turnover. *Journal of Accountancy*, June, pp. 86-88.

Whittington, G. 1995. Is Accounting Becoming Too Interesting? Sir Julian Hodge Lecture, University of Wales, Aberystwyth.

Wilensky, H.L. 1964. The professionalization of everyone? *American Journal of Sociology*, September, pp. 137-158.

Willmott, H., P. Sikka and A. Puxty. 1994. Barely afloat: The industrialisation and self-regulation of accounting. *The Journal of Applied Accounting Research*, No.1, pp. 58-79.

Winch, P. 1958. *The Idea of a Social Science and its Relationship to Philosophy*, Routledge & Kegan Paul.

Wolfe, D.M. and J.D. Snoek. 1962. A study of tension and adjustment under role conflict. *Journal of Social Issues*, July, pp. 102-121.

Wright, A. 1980. Performance appraisal of staff auditors. *The CPA Journal*, November, pp. 37-43.

Wright, A. 1982. Investigation of the engagement evaluation process for staff auditors. *Journal of Accounting Research*, Spring, pp. 227-239.

Wright, A. 1985. Rating the raters: Indications of senior' performance in evaluating staff auditors. *Advances in Accounting*, pp. 185-198.

Wright, A. 1986. Performance evaluation of staff auditors: A behaviourally anchored rating scale. *Auditing: A Journal of Practice & Theory*, Spring, pp. 95-108.

Wright, A. 1988. The comparative performance of MBAs vs. undergraduate accounting majors in public accounting. *The Accounting Review*, January, pp. 123-136.

Wyman, P. 1997. No training, no future. *Accountancy*, October, pp. 72-73.

Yukl, G.A. 1989. Managerial leadership: A review of theory and research. *Journal of Management*, June, pp. 251-289.

$$$ Zytowski, D.G. and R. Hay. 1994. Do birds of a feather flock together? A test of the similarities within and the differences between five occupations. *Journal of Vocational Behaviour*, April, pp. 242-248.